Thank you...
To my parents for always believing in me.
To the followers of my blog: You've been loyal since the beginning.
To Mrs. Jackson: You gave me fuel for the fire that is my writing. You told me I'd never be good enough and to stop being so foolish.
Again, to my parents for teaching me to be my own person and to have enough strength not to listen to people like Mrs. Jackson.
To my wonderful children for letting me be your mom.
Last but not least, thank you to my husband. Without you, I would have no stories. Worse yet, I would have no one to share any stories with. Thanks for telling me I could do this, forcing me to work when I had a mental block, and throwing a pizza in the oven when I was preoccupied. I love you.

INTRODUCTION

The ebb and flow of the inner workings of agriculture follow the seasons. Life on a ranch is dictated by the changing of the seasons. A yearly calendar doesn't hold much relevance in this line of work. This book reflects that. The start of my life as a ranch wife was in the fall so that seemed as good of a place as any to begin. So while some of my stories might not be in chronological order, they are in the natural order. The way things happen naturally on a ranch. The seasons demand it to be so.

FALL

A chill is on the breeze. Damp leaves spice the air. There is a ringing sound of freshly-weaned calves yearning for mother's milk. The loud bawl of cows needing to dry up lingers heavily. The warmth of horseflesh growing a winter coat. The miles put on a saddle from the long gathers. The rush of preparations before the snow flies.

"I don't think you're tough enough to be a ranch wife."

1

GATHERING

I stood next to my new husband of one whole month and stared at the computer screen. He had found a help wanted ad for a ranch about two hours away and informed me we were headed for an interview. It was October with cool weather in the air and the threat of snow ever present. The next morning was the first time I set foot on a working ranch.

We stood on the doorstep of a 96-year-old man's home. My Cowboy did all the talking while my mind was reeling. I couldn't help but think that I was the polar opposite of the weathered man that stood stooped at his walker in front of me. I would eventually learn that thought was just the tip of those polar icebergs. I had much to learn to become a ranch wife.

Our first week at the ranch was memorable in more ways than one. It started by blowing out three tires while transporting our belongings in a ranch stock trailer. I wasn't familiar with this mode of moving transportation but, trust me, it's the norm in ranching communities. Then the move peaked while cleaning out our new residence so as to free it from nasty and stained broken furniture, random chicken bones sporadically placed under said furniture and on top of the refrigerator, and a "funk" smell that arose from the shag carpets that permeated the entire house. In case there was any question, yes, I was wondering what I had gotten myself into by falling in love with a cowboy. The week was culminated by a drive with Ray.

Our first day on the job was slightly less physically strenuous but no less stressful than the actual move in. The boss, Ray, was eager to show us around so we could get the lay of his land. We piled in his single cab Ford truck and began the journey with a 96-year-old at the wheel. He showed us pastures, fence lines, and property borders. It was while we were on the main roads that an interesting point was brought up. Ray had his driver's license taken away several years before. I can't think of a worse time to find out such information. We were miles from home and in unfamiliar country. We were at his mercy. Looking back, I now know this was all a part of Ray's plan from the beginning. He was like that, full of mischief.

Before heading to Ray's "mountain ground", which is a general term for summer pastures in mountain ranges often times being comprised of government land leases, we switched everyone over to our pickup truck complete with a legal driver. We bounced an empty stock trailer up the dirt roads so we could eventually put a wayward steer in it. Ray was proud to show us all of his pastures and introduced us to the neighbors who corralled the fence-jumping steer we were after. With just a short visit, we were back on the road.

Ray then pointed us up another dirt road. He wanted to show us the point where the cows would be turned out in the spring and, in essence, make a big loop around the mountain to end up only a short distance from the ranch come fall time. Unknown to us, there must have been some good rain in the area recently or perhaps even some mountain snow. At any rate, the road was wet. Muddy, to be precise. We made our way pretty far up this road with a mostly-wild steer in the back dancing around all the while. At some point my husband's better judgment kicked in and he suggested to our new boss we should turn around. We finally were able to do so with quite an effort and a bit of "off the road and into the sage-brush" technique.

The ride out was the worst part of this whole adventure. Where we had slipped around in the mud on the way in, we now spun our tires in ruts on the way out. As we began to cross what appeared to be an old washout, my eyes were slightly enlarged. I was on the "hospital" side, as they say, and looking down a fairly large draw. It was big enough to make a truck and trailer flip over at least once if a mistake was made.

I watched out the window as we began to slide backwards. The trailer was starting to slide into the draw, taking the truck with it. A few seconds went by of gear switching, gas pedal mashing, steering wheel turning, cowboy cussing, and turbo diesel testing that resulted in us on drier ground plowing through sagebrush and breathing a sigh of relief. It took a bit longer for the color to come back to my knuckles.

The man who led us on this misadventure then made a profound statement. Since he was only a month away from turning 97 years old it held special meaning. With a sly grin, Ray said, "That's probably the stupidest idea I've ever had."

The next couple of days were spent organizing, cleaning and getting to know the ranch. We also made time to check the fences and ride the pastures. It was then we noticed we needed to move the herd to better grass.

Up until this point, I had only been around roping steers or calves, which are considerably smaller than your average cow, within the confines of an arena. Sometimes I was on a horse and other times I was on foot just walking behind them getting them to go into the roping chutes; still nothing very extensive. Certainly nothing that anyone would call real experience.

Riding my trusty steed Tango, I was told by the Cowboy, "Just stay behind them and keep them moving." I was full of questions but he gave no answers as he rode off. The cows knew more than I did and headed for the gate without much of my help.

Occasionally the Cowboy knows best but let's not let that get out or back to him. He knew I just needed to do it, to learn it. I wasn't a professional by any means but I had moved my first bunch of cows and it went off without a hitch.

During the first week of working for Ray, I thought I would have time to start unpacking my house. I guess I was being silly when I thought that. It was fall and the cows had only been back on the ranch for a couple weeks when the neighbor called. He'd just gathered off the mountain and was short one bull. He gave us the make and model - you know, the size, breed, and tag number - and we were off hunting a bull. The Cowboy told me to check the lower part of the pasture by the river while he took the far corner. We were supposed to work our way back to the barn so everything was covered.

For those of you keeping track, this was the second time I'd moved or even been around cattle that were not in an arena. I'd never had to move a bull; heck, I'd never really even seen one that close before. As usual, I was a ball of nerves as I took a deep breath and kicked my horse forward. All the terrible stories I'd heard were flooding back through my head. What if he charges my horse? What if he won't move? What if he does try to take my horse and I get bucked off and stomped to death with no one around to help since my dear loving husband apparently doesn't give a crap about my well-being since he left me to fend for myself???? These really are the things that go through my head, no joke.

I was getting stiff as a board on top of my horse so I started singing.... "Please don't find this bull. Wherever you are, don't be here because I don't want to find you."....you get the idea. This went on through a few meadows, some trees, and a couple creek crossings. CRAP . . . there he was. I didn't sing loud enough I guess. I pointed my horse so we could get a better look. Yup, for sure, it was him; the brand and numbers matched. I sat there and debated for a bit. Would it be obvious if I just rode right past him? Could I play the "never done this before" card? Hmmm, this was a tough one.

I swallowed hard like a cartoon "gulp" and bumped my horse forward. I didn't want to be out here all day chasing a bull around just because I let this chance pass me by right now. He was huge - at least he seemed huge to me - he was snorty, and he wasn't moving. I finally got him to stand up at least from all the yelling and hollering I was doing. I figured if nothing else, the Cowboy might hear me and think I was in trouble and come to my rescue. Umm, yeah... not so much.

I finally had the bull on the move after much yelling, waving and horse maneuvering. We had a long way to go that was made even longer since the bull had no sense of direction. I think it's bred into them to not walk a straight line, to always turn around to see if you're still there; in general, just be pissy and overall stress me out. So you can imagine all the fun I had with this bull from that last statement. Thankfully, my horse didn't freak out at all this; only I did.

I'm almost to the gate. What do I do now? The

Cowboy was supposed to have been here and opened the gate for me; at least that's how it went in my head. Great, now I have to open a gate where there's cows hanging out, get back on my horse (with my short legs and fat butt, this is a great accomplishment on a good day all by itself), gather the bull back up without the cows, and get him through the gate and up to the corrals. Hmm, I thought I had problems before. So I set out to get all the steps done in the shortest amount of time. Surprisingly, it goes off without a hitch. Just as I close the gate behind the bull (minus any extra cows), guess who shows up? Riding up like the Lone Ranger coming to save the day was my Cowboy.

"Look what I did all by myself! Where have you been?" was all I had to say. He then explained his whereabouts. He was watching me the whole time. He wanted me to do something on my own so I knew I could do it by myself. He told me he was proud of me and I did a good job. I wonder what he would have said if his sneaky plan backfired because I was too chicken and just rode past the bull!

Oh well, I guess the Cowboy is right when he says, "Do a good job because you never know who's watching."

2

WEANING

I t felt like any other day when the Cowboy roused me out of my warm bed. The time had come for us to wean the calves. Unlike some other places that wean and then ship their calves off to the sale, we were at Ray's and that meant keeping our calves to raise as yearlings and then sell.

The Cowboy had a plan of action that would be set into motion as soon as I had put on my trusty Carhart coveralls and walked out the door with coffee in hand and cigarette in mouth. Gross, I know, but I was young and thought it was a good idea at the time. I started my four-wheeler and followed the Cowboy; we had gathered the cows the day before so now they were in a small pasture right next to the corrals. We opened the gate and buzzed in with the four-wheelers. The cows and calves were in the corrals in just a few minutes.

Now came the stressful part for me. I had never sorted anything before, on a horse or on foot. Needless to say, the Cowboy didn't exactly trust my abilities to cut a cow on a horse so he opted for sorting on foot. He figured if all else failed, I could swing a gate. I soon realized exactly how big cows are when you aren't on a horse. I was petrified.

I can't even tell you how many times I cried that morning. I screamed. I cried. I yelled. I cried. I fell. I cried. I swung a gate. I cried. I let a calf go by. I cried. I wasn't sure if I was crying over being sad, mad, or just frustrated. I'm sure it was all of the above at every given second.

The Cowboy was doing a good job sorting everything. All I had to do was open or shut the gate, depending on what was coming my way. Sounds easy enough, right? Well, this is what should have happened.

Cow coming: Open the gate, stand back and let her go through and down the alley, close the gate, don't let any calves down the alley.

Calf coming: Close the gate, run to the opposite side of the corrals, open that gate, help push calves into that pen, close gate.

This is what actually happened.

Cow coming: Open the gate, when cow looks at me run for the fence, abandon gate responsibilities, get yelled at for previous actions, cry, scream, wipe tears so I can see the cow coming at me again, open gate again while screaming like little girl, let calf through because I didn't close gate fast enough, now jump the fence like a fat girl and try to run down the alley to catch calf before he mixes in with the rest of the cows while still crying and now cussing. Repeat for next cow.

Calf coming: Leave cow gate slightly open thinking that cows don't have thumbs so it will be fine because you don't have time to actually latch it with calves coming at you, waddle to the calf gate because nicotine and winter fat is hampering running abilities if I ever had any to begin with, get yelled at for taking too long, scream and cry, open gate, get yelled at for being in the way, scream and cuss, get calves to go through the calf gate and not the cow gate that they are trying to go through because it's slightly more open than when I left it, waddle with a slight hurry to close calf gate behind calves only because you don't want to go through it all again, latch gate this time. Walk back to cow gate out of breath, screaming that the cow can wait, craving another cigarette.

It was a long morning that I was happy to see an end to. The cows were back in the nearby pasture, some were grazing, most were bellowing for their calves. The calves were in the corrals bawling their little faces off. They could still see and smell each other through the corrals but couldn't nurse. I couldn't believe how loud it all was. The Cowboy assured me it would go on for at least a day but probably more. We headed to the house for some lunch.

After lunch, we came back to the shop to do some maintenance on some of the equipment for the afternoon. I was busy organizing, sweeping and singing to the radio. The Cowboy was busy doing manly stuff.

Then it hit me. It was really quiet. I asked the Cowboy, "I thought you said they'd bawl for a couple days?" Then it hit him.

We hopped on a four-wheeler and buzzed over to where the corrals and pasture met. Everyone was accounted for but not in their proper place. All the calves were sucking milk to their heart's content and to their mother's relief. My heart sank. The calves managed to get the gate open and we would have to sort all over again. Not only was it the longest morning of my life, now it was going to be the longest day of my life.

No, I wasn't any braver the second time around. There were still cows looking at me funny. I was even less enthused about running to gates. There was more crying and cussing, much more. It was a hard way to learn how to sort cattle. It was an even harder way to learn that it's a good idea to just wire the gate shut, or better yet, wean your calves far, far, far, far, far, far, far, far, far, far, far, far, far away from the cows.

The Cowboy was right though; they did bawl for days. At that time, all I could think of was that they were making it hard for me to sleep. Now, I welcome the sound. I know it's just a cow being a good momma and every herd could use more of those.

3

SHIPPING

Friday:

I woke up that morning not to the usual sounds of "Momma, Momma" through the baby monitor but that of my husband saying hurry up and catch your horse. Sigh. I remembered mornings like this, the days before children. My munchkin was at Ga-gaw and Paw-paw's house for the weekend so I could help out the Cowboy on the ranch. We had a big weekend ahead of us and we knew it would be some long days.

We had a few other people coming to help us. There was the usual: my Cowboy, the other ranch-hand, and four more besides myself. Well, due to injuries from dealing with horses the day before, our crew ended up only five strong. This meant I was able to ride my old man Tango. I was going to pass him off to a lady that's been ranching much longer than I and could use a good easy ride. I was sad that she couldn't come along but glad to have my trusty steed, too.

We headed out to gather and find a dry corner to sort from. In that area, by mid-summer, some of the pastures turned to giant soggy bogs. Partly from irrigation but mostly from the water table being high. Before we could pick out our corner, we had to cross a bog. Now, call it fear, call it smarts, call it whatever you want, but I wasn't going first. There were four other guys that could find a good place to cross and I'd follow the driest!

The Cowboy was the first to go, the first to start sinking and the first to start spurring to keep moving forward to get out. His horse had mud up to her belly. I didn't follow him. The next two went with not much more luck than the first. I watched the ground move in waves with every step their horse took. It was like walking an 1100 pound animal over a water bed that you'd randomly sink in. Then the Cowboy was telling me where to come across. The last of the guys went near where I was being told to go and he didn't sink too far. So I started across this bog. I was told to, "Give him his head." So I tossed the reins, grabbed the saddle horn in my right hand, the cantle with my left, sunk my butt in the middle and kept spurring all through half-closed eyes. I didn't want to watch but had to in case I had to bail if my horse got stuck. I did however hold my breath.

Once we were all safe and sound and on dry ground, the Cowboy formed a plan. We all got our marching orders and had a plan of attack. A while after we rode to our respective places, the cows were balling up on their own in a different corner. So like other things, you have to roll with the punches and change plans. Just do what you need to do to get the job done. So everyone adjusted and soon we were all back together with the herd in a corner and ready to sort.

My job was to hold the herd. Luckily for me, I wasn't alone; I had help from two other guys. We were constantly chasing the brave ones that would try to break out. There was one big red cow that was sneaky and would walk really slow and not make eye contact. She almost made it three or four times. She'd just go back into the herd and make her way around to try the next guy. It was pretty funny to watch her.

It seemed like it took forever to get everything sorted into their proper places. Basically, we had to sort off about 100 head of young cows who didn't have calves that would be staying on the ranch and leave the other 200 cows with calves. This way, on shipping day, we wouldn't have as many to sort through. It only felt like forever since it was so hot out. We then had to put the one group in a different pasture.

On our way to push the cows, we stopped in the creek to water the horses. There was water, water everywhere and not a decent drop to drink. I was dying of thirst. A couple of the guys did a quick head dunk in the water to cool off. Silly boys, if I would have done that I would have smelled like a creek for weeks. I'd never get the fish smell out of my hair. Plus the fact that my entire back would have been soaking wet; maybe I'm just still too much of a girl. Hard telling.

After moving the young cows into the correct pasture, we had to doctor a lump jaw cow. When I say "we", I mean them. I'm not afraid to say that doctoring cows in the pasture is not my forte. I can handle calves in the pasture or cows in a chute but that's about it. So I stayed out of the way as they got the job done. First, the cow was roped by her head and then the Cowboy caught her two back feet. Then the ground crew came in. This isn't always available but it's nice to have a couple extra guys. That way the ropers don't have to get off their horses and they can make sure to keep the ropes tight which keeps the guys on the ground safe.

There were a few comments about how this ground crew wouldn't cut the mustard on a ranch rodeo team because they were taking too long. It was all in good fun though. They got the job done and the cow was no worse for the wear and better for the doctoring.

By this time, I was so thirsty I was tempted to drink ditch water. Tempted, but I didn't actually do it…gross. I knew we were headed back to the trailer anyway. I don't know if you have heard the saying that pretty much any crisis can be solved with the contents of a ranch truck but it stands true. I dug around and found a couple jugs of water in the truck. Wahoo! We put the horses in the trailer and were off to find more liquid and some lunch. Then it was on to the usual irrigating and then calling it a day.

Saturday:

The day started a little later than the one before. We didn't have to gather anything so we weren't out of bed and catching horses at 6:00am. I can't even tell you how happy I was about this. Our first weekend without a munchkin and there really wasn't much sleeping happening. Such is life.

The Cowboy and I thought it would be a good idea to stop in and have coffee with some friends of ours to start the day. Before we could do that, we had to feed some critters. As we drove to the other end of the ranch, I noticed there were some extra horses in the neighbor's pasture. I said, "That's a nice looking horse. When did they get new horses?" The Cowboy took a look and announced, "They're ours."

Now for fear of making myself sound like a fry short of a happy meal, let me explain. By "ours" he meant the ranch. I do know my horses when I see them. The ranch horses I didn't see every day. They were mostly two- and three-year-olds that haven't been trained with one or two old horses that didn't get used anymore. Twelve horses standing in the neighbor's pasture isn't something you want to see first thing in the morning. This is especially true when the only way to get them home is to load them into a trailer.

While I gave the Cowboy my usual 50 questions,

we fed the sheep. Most of the sheep were turned out to pasture but there were a few older ewes that needed a little extra feed and lambs that were already full-grown and would be sold for meat. I pointed out a lamb that had prolapsed to the Cowboy and he went to inspect it. He didn't have any luck fixing it right then so we'd have to come back later with the proper tools and medicine to get the little bugger straightened out. After four buckets of grain, hay pitched in the racks, and water filled up, we were on our way to get a trailer and deal with the renegade horses.

It wasn't too long before we had the trailer hooked on and some extra help from the other ranch hand. By this time, the neighbor was nice enough to open the gate to the corrals and our bunch filed right in. We had enough room in the trailer for all of them but it didn't exactly work out that way.

The Cowboy caught the old horse, which was feeling mighty frisky, and tried to do the old bait and shut the trailer door trick. That only worked on a couple of the yearling horses. So after a few failed attempts and much dust in the air, we went to get a few panels. The helper dropped off the few horses we managed to trick into our corrals while the Cowboy and I loaded up panels.

Once the panels were set correctly and the trailer was backed up, away we went. We got around the horses, they went into the smaller pen of panels, we slowly brought the panels smaller and smaller, and... Voila! They were in the trailer! Easy peasy! We unloaded the bunch into the corrals without a fuss. Now we had a date with a lamb.

I've learned that ranchers usually add veterinarian to their list of qualifications. Of course this isn't official but a general knowledge of doctoring is a must in this occupation. So in case you didn't know what a prolapse is, I'll break it down for you. There are a few types that I know of but I'll just explain the most common types. There's a uterine prolapse that happens while giving birth; this is where the uterus comes out after the baby is born so the uterus is basically inside out. This can be partial or complete. There is a vaginal prolapse that can happen any time; this is where the inner wall of the vagina will protrude. There is also an anal prolapse; this is where the lining of the rectum protrudes. I'm sure there's more in depth descriptions but you get the idea.

Since we were dealing with a lamb, the fix for this anal prolapse was a little trickier. On an anal-prolapsed cow, you numb the area, push everything back in and stitch it back into place, more or less. Well, the Cowboy has all the necessary equipment to work on a cow but sheep are considerably smaller. I don't think the lamb would have appreciated it one bit! Lucky for us, the ranch owner we worked for at that time was a vet. Unlucky for us, he was out of town. So, after a quick phone conversation, we had our marching orders.

Turns out, there was no stitching required. We cleaned the area, I held his feet, and the Cowboy went to stuffing things back to where they belonged. Then to get the "stuffing" to stay put, a few little shots were needed. Basically, sheep have a mild allergic reaction to Oxytetracycline, otherwise known as Biomycin or LA 200, the "go to" broad spectrum antibiotic that no ranch is without. So if you give a few little shots of it around the anus, the tissue will swell slightly and keep the insides, well, inside. Then eventually scar tissue will develop and no more prolapse. However, there are some times when this doesn't work and you will have to resort to stitching. So while this lamb might be the laughingstock of all his friends for having a swollen rump, at least he's alive and healthy with all his "innards".

The day continued on without much of a hitch. We went around some fence, fixed the hole that the horses crawled out of, and mended a few other spots. We then headed to the corrals to do a little patching and preparation to make ready for the next two days of sorting and shipping.

Sunday:

Sunday was an early morning, beginning at 5:00am. We were catching horses when one thought it would be a great idea to be a turd. So many minutes later than planned, we finally had the horses saddled up, loaded in the trailer and ready to go. A friend of ours was meeting us at our house and helping us today. All together there would be six of us.

The plan for the day was to gather everything besides the young cows we sorted on Friday. After gathering, we'd then sort off most of the calves and some cows, all of which would be headed to the sale. The trucks were coming at 10:00am so we allowed more than enough time for everything. You never know though. It's been said before; when things go bad on a ranch...they go really bad. After all that, we still would have to go to the other end of the ranch and trail about 150 pairs closer to home. It's only a few miles but we did have to trail down part of the road and then cross it.

Things were going well on the gather, no major problems. The calves were slow as always but at least they were staying together. They crossed the river and headed into the next pasture like good little kids. It was a little harder to get them through that pasture into the corrals though. The grass was tall and green so they didn't want to move very much but we eventually got them to the corrals. The calves, of course, kept trying to turn back but that's to be expected. A giant dust cloud was beginning to form as we started up the wooden plank fence alley that funneled the cows into the corrals. It wasn't looking promising for the rest of the day to be dust free.

Now came the fun part, sorting. The calves only broke out once and it was at the very beginning so no major harm done. I've learned this process is much easier with several people! Soon we finally had all the calves sorted off and we were ready to fill trucks. The first truck showed up at about 9:30. Good thing we allowed extra time; otherwise we would have been running behind the eight ball. The trucks were early but we were ready.

After all the sorting, loading, and everything was shipped, we loaded up the horses and headed out to trail the rest of the cows home. We stopped to eat some pizza on the tailgate of the truck and guzzle down massive amounts of fluid. The dust was killing all of us and we were covered in it. No one would let me take pictures of their dirty faces but we all looked like we got locked in a tanning booth for a week.

We headed out into the sagebrush and got them pointed in the right direction. On my way to bring a pair, my horse started freaking out. He was hopping around and then trying to bolt. I was confused for a second until I heard the culprit. No, thank God, it wasn't a snake or else I would have freaked out more than he did! His back feet were caught in wire. He was dragging it and it was pulling tight and popping in the sagebrush. You can put anything around this horse's feet and he's fine. But wire just freaks him out and he just flips his gourd and loses his mind. Luckily, he's not a bronc and you can talk him out of most anything. I hopped off, untangled his legs, checked everything out, and all was well. No cuts, no blood.

We had everything gathered in no time and it was time to cross the canal. This was the irrigation canal. It's about eight feet across, chest deep on a horse - three to four feet - and it has very steep sides that are a few feet tall. I've never had to cross water quite like this before. As you might have guessed, I wasn't the first to cross. Again, the Cowboy found a good spot for me; still I had to kick my feet out of my stirrups and lift my feet so I didn't get soaked.

The rest of the gather and trail went well. When we were on the road, a bull went AWOL. He went through, not over, the neighbor's fence. So the rest of the boys went to gather up the bull while the Cowboy and I continued with the herd. We were on the home-stretch anyway so it wasn't a big deal. Just as we were pushing all the rest of the cows into the pasture, here came the bull, finally.

Monday:

Monday morning, I again was awakened by "Momma, Momma, Momma". The munchkin's long weekend with the grandparents came to an end Sunday evening. It was wonderful to have her back home but that meant I couldn't help out the Cowboy. The sorting and shipping was happening all over again with the bunch of cows that we trailed home the day before. He started them on his own with his dog and headed for the corrals. He had to go through five pastures to get there and help was meeting him in the middle.

The trucks arrived empty and left full. There were a few extra that wouldn't fit so the Cowboy and I hauled them over to the sale barn. The next day was the sale.

Tuesday:

The Cowboy had to sort and drop off some bulls in the morning but then we were headed to the sale barn. We went into the cafe for a bite to eat before the sale. It brought back memories of my Uncle Fritz. The Cowboy and I sat with him in the cafe many times before the sale. We were there buying and selling for Ray and my uncle was the auctioneer at the sale barn that my Grandaddy built. Good talks, good food, and even better pie.

Anyway, the sale was good. The calves sold well. We didn't stay to watch the older cows sell because we had to gather up a stray bull that was at the neighbor's corrals. So all was well and then we were waiting on a bunch of fall calves to arrive to feed through the winter. The fences weren't ready to run yearlings. Oh well, such is life. Besides, without the fun of bad fences, I wouldn't have near as many stories to pass on to my kids.

4

FILLING THE FREEZER

Hunting is an important way of life for all the ranches I've known. Many ranch freezers are stocked for the winter with wild game. The Cowboy and I, on more than one occasion, have relied on hunting different animals to keep us fed through the cold winter months. Most of the hunting trips are enjoyable and uneventful but one time it led to a little bit of cabin fever.

I watched the Cowboy ride away on the four-wheeler and wondered how long it would be until I saw him again. My three-year-old munchkin was pointing out how messy the old cabin was as she stood in her blue and white socks that looked like ballerina slippers. Of all days to forget a pair of shoes, it just had to be today. We were cold and alone; now what?

We left the house that morning at about 6 am. It was still dark outside and only a bit nippy. I went to grab my coat and the Cowboy informed me that it wasn't cold. I did anyway. I woke up the munchkin, wrapped her in blankets and took her straight to the truck. After a quick buckle-up, she was soon bundled back up in her blankies and snug as a bug. There was no going back to sleep for her once I told her we were going hunting for antelope. She has been talking about it for weeks. She even asked for her own gun, a pink one of course.

Within two hours of leaving the house, we were up on the mountain into our hunting area and we were loading up a doe onto the truck. It also happens to be bird season in that same area. We drove around some more until he came to a draw where he'd seen several game birds hanging out. He never forgets where all the wild game are when he's out gathering cows or in search of cows. I think it's a male thing because I only have this sense every once in a while. It is funny how he can rarely remember where other things are when he needs them; also a male thing.

He zipped off on the four-wheeler in search of the mighty sage grouse aka the prairie chicken. He soon returned with one in hand. We then drove around some more and decided to head into cow camp and make some coffee since the Cowboy was fresh out already. Where we were hunting was the same area as the ranch's summer leases. The Cowboy and I had been in that area off and on all summer long with the cows so we had a chance to keep the cow camp stocked with a few bare necessities. On our way there something terrible happened. The transmission on one of the ranch trucks went completely out.

Hmmmm, ok great! Sagebrush to the left and right, bluffs and buttes in the distance, dirt road in the middle, and the nearest "town" that consisted of only a few houses and a bar was 20 miles away and it didn't open till noon.

I calmly suggested to a very aggravated Cowboy that he take the munchkin and I the rest of the way into cow camp on the four-wheeler and then he could go to town to call for help. A brisk and slightly wet couple of miles on the four-wheeler later, all the while the munchkin wrapped in blankies and telling me "This is fun, Mommy," we pulled into cow camp. It's funny how oblivious kids are to some things. I gave my coat to the Cowboy and assured him we'd be fine. He headed for town.

I looked around and there were only big pieces of wood that were dry, nothing to actually start a fire. So with the munchkin on my back we headed to find something, anything small, dry and flammable. Finally, I found the mother lode hidden under the more than one-hundred-year-old barn's petticoats. Pieces of wooden shingles and various other pieces of wood were all safe and dry. You just had to dig a little through all the years of livestock "leavings" but it all burned the same.

I headed back to the cabin with an armload of wood and a monkey on my back while it again started to sprinkle on us. I quickly got the fire started without many problems at all. The bigger pieces weren't taking off quite like I was hoping so a trip back to the barn was in order. I settled the munchkin in a chair. She was happily playing games on my phone that had not an ounce of reception. By this time, it was raining so I threw a blanket around me to keep warm and dry for the trek to the barn. Walking was all that could happen because there was no running with my seven-month pregnant belly.

Before I made the trek to the barn, I grabbed the bag that went to the fold-up chairs in the cabin so I could carry more wood at once. I was quickly picking up wood and muttering to myself that I'd better not get this thing full only to find the Cowboy coming over the hill to our rescue. Back to the cabin I went but by now it was pouring rain and all I could think was "poor Cowboy". He was speeding down the road on a four-wheeler in the pouring rain - I'm talking buckets here - in a coat that had no buttons, was only made of one layer of fleece material, and the ugliest red and black colors made to look like a terrible knock-off of a Navajo blanket.

In the meantime, the munchkin and I were toasty warm in a hand-chinked, mouse-infested, 10x15, well over one hundred-year-old cabin. Even in the places that you could see daylight, it was still nice and toasty with my roaring fire. I didn't care if I was there for an hour or half the day, I was stoking that fire!

A few hours later when the Cowboy pulled up in a different ranch truck, the munchkin and I had just finished an apple and no one jumped up to greet him. I saw him coming down the hill but didn't want to leave my cozy spot by the fire. He walked in, found us cozy and immediately walked over to warm up by the fire. He then confessed that it was a bit of a letdown to find us doing so well. He was thinking that we'd be in a state of unrest and rush out to greet him, the conquering hero come to our rescue. He even said, "There I was feeling guilty about sitting in the warm restaurant waiting for help to get here with the other ranch truck, having left my girls to fend for themselves."

Even if it wasn't a matter of life and death, I was quite proud of my survival skills to keep the munchkin and I safe and sound. I wasn't about to admit to him that it was partly his fault. All these years on the ranch, he'd taught me to be smart, get things done because no one was going to do it for you, and not to give up because there were lives depending on you. I just kept thinking how others might have freaked out in such a situation and that made me happy. Twisted, I know. That's the difference between those that think they can handle going from city girl to ranch wife and those of us that actually do.

WILD GAME ISN'T THE ONLY MEAT IN OUR FREEZER. I'VE learned to like lamb, crave our home-raised pork, and appreciate a free range chicken. Sometimes we've had beef as one of our salary benefits and we've gone without as well. There are many reasons why I like to eat beef. I grew up in a house where we had a variety of meals as well as meats. I'm not nearly as "dyed in the wool" about beef as my husband is, but I do enjoy it. In fact, many of my favorite meals growing up were some sort of beef dish.

By now it's no surprise that I did not grow up seeing beef on the hoof, much less looking it in the eye. I will admit it was an adjustment to come face to face with a food source. There are things in this ranch life that make it easier though. By the time we fed our first steer, took him to the packing house, and brought him home to our freezer, I was well over any issues I might have had.

It might have helped that I named him Pork Chop and he hated me. Even if I brought a bucket of grain and armfuls of hay, he still chased me out of the pen. Well, when something hates you and tries to harm you, it does make it easier to enjoy them in the form of a steak. That was an easy lesson to learn; a tasty one, too.

I still have some issues with the idea of veal though. I've eaten it before but just the thought kind of freaked me out. I think it's because I have the image of a newborn calf on my dinner plate. I know this isn't the case. A 450-pound calf is very far from newborns. It's just hard to think of when you're bottle-feeding that bum calf with those big doe eyes. Well, one day I quickly got over my issues with eating veal.

I went with the Cowboy to load up a few calves and two cows that wouldn't fit on the trucks the day before to take to the sale. Not a big deal, just like any other time we've hauled cows to the sale barn. The Cowboy backed up the trailer to the chute. We wired a panel to the one side and the door of the trailer served as the barrier on the other side. Like clockwork, two cows loaded up and right behind them were five "heavy" or big calves. I started to swing the panel so that the Cowboy could start to shut the trailer door. That's about when calf #6 had the idea to duck his head under the panel. This bald-faced steer weighed in at about 550 pounds. I was told to get in front of him so I took about two steps to do so.

Right about here is when it all went downhill fast. The calf bulldozed his way under the panel and started to head for the hills. This action caused the reaction, or rather lack of reaction, on my part. The panel hit me in the back of the knees and completely swept me off my feet. I landed on my shoulders, thwacked my head and my elbow, too. My foot was caught up in the panel and was squished after I was drug for a quick second.

I rolled over and scrambled away, giving a quick mental sigh when I saw the Cowboy shut the trailer door so I wasn't in any more danger. He quickly came over to help me up. I couldn't catch my breath enough to sob as much as I wanted to. Holy Crap on a cracker Batman! That hurt. I wailed like a baby. My Cowboy helped me to the truck, dusted me off, and called in reinforcements. The calf was halfway across the pasture now, mixed in with a different bunch of calves and still had to get in the trailer.

Twenty minutes later, he was loaded and we were on our way to the sale barn. Six hours later I was still crying and in pain. My Cowboy again helped me into the truck and we went to see a doctor. Luckily, nothing was broken. My ankle was badly sprained and my elbow was deeply bruised. Even years later, on a cold day, my elbow and halfway down my arm still shows where the purple bruise was.

When all this happened, if I could have I would have shot, skinned, cut and wrapped that steer all by myself. I think I ate beef all week while I gimped around on my wrapped foot, now that I think about it. I do remember looking through my cookbook for things like Veal Parmigiana and Veal Marsala just out of pure spite.

I know it's not the most noble of reasons to eat beef. I don't even think it would make a good commercial for why to eat more beef. I bet if you were there, you'd know what I mean. Talk about a guilt-free hamburger. I'm never thinking twice about eating any form of beef again.

WINTER

The cold winds that blow in a blizzard, freeze up water tanks, and take all the energy out of you while you take care of your animals can be life-altering. The calm of big fluffy snowflakes falling onto the backs of livestock happily eating hay in sunshine while you breathe it all in is life-affirming. The thought of not having either one of those experiences, to me, would be life-shattering.

"Just think of all the stories we will have to tell our children."

FIRST LESSONS

Ranch life is full of lessons. I think if you stop learning something from it, it must be because you're dead. My first few lessons on the ranch were just as the snow was starting to fly and all involved yearlings in one stage or another. Sometimes the lesson is to appreciate the help you have while it's there. Other times it's just to enjoy life and laugh a little. Then there's times when the lesson is hard to swallow and heart-wrenching.

Help Lesson:

Just when I thought I had learned a few things about moving cows, the rules were all of a sudden changed. I didn't realize this was possible. At this point, to me a cow was a cow, bovine was bovine. With the exceptions of a few "wild eyed" ones, you used pretty much the same techniques to move them around. Get behind or around them and push them forward. Stay at the hip to drive, come to the shoulder to stop or turn. The Cowboy repeatedly told me about these imaginary lines.

So one terribly cold, windy, freezing rain and snowy day, both the Cowboy and I had some lessons coming that we didn't know about. We had trucks coming that afternoon to load yearlings and take to the sale. The help consisted of me and the Cowboy, one dog that still didn't really know what she was doing, and an old man in a pickup truck vs. 500 yearling bovines. I set out that morning like I did most others, moving a little slow but moving all the same. I didn't think much about what we were going to do; I knew the plan. Take them out of their current pasture, through the gate at the corner, into the horse pasture, around the barn, and up into the sorting corrals. It really wasn't that far to go either. The Cowboy had warned me to keep them moving because they'd have a tendency to turn back, more so than a cow.

We were all ready to go and had opened and shut the proper gates to make for an easy gather and push. Well, if you think that's how it went, you've never moved yearlings. The minute we stepped a horse's hoof through that gate, their tails went in the air. Those little buggers went from quietly munching hay to land-speed record-holding bovines in the matter of seconds. We'd rode through them several times before without so much as a strange look. I'm convinced that any type of livestock just knows when you're on a schedule. So instead of pushing them straight to the gate, now we have to ride to the opposite end of a 500-acre pasture, let the buggers settle down, then get them back to the starting point.

Some of these were "our" calves that were home-raised on the ranch and some were outside calves that were bought in the previous fall. As I'm on my horse, trying to get these turds to head for the gate, I'm scolding them like a mean kindergarten teacher. "I see you there; you're not sneaky, get back in line!" "Speed it up buddy, you're getting left behind." "You take one more step....don't even think about turning around, mister!"

It was not going well to say the least. If you've never moved yearlings, I recommend you try to get out of it at all costs. They were scattered as if you dropped a handful of rubber bouncy balls on a school gym floor. We tried several different methods when one after another kept failing. That's one thing about the Cowboy I admire. He keeps at it until it's done, trying something fifty different ways till he finds the one that works. Maybe it comes from the way he works with horses; one thing doesn't always work for the next, so you have to figure out what that horse needs to be successful. Anyway, that was just me bragging for a minute.

So back to the bouncy balls, well, they were still bouncing. Just as we'd get them close to the gate and a few were going through, "something" would happen to break their concentration, or whatever happens in a yearling bovine brain, and they would all spill back on us. That something was...dat-da-da-dahh, Ray to the rescue! I guess with his eyesight, they were all through the gate and he didn't want to get left behind. He'd stomp on the gas to catch up only to find all the calves running back at him. Thank goodness he backed off after only a couple times of that but it wasn't soon enough for our liking. So we still have 500 of these fur-balls running in every direction.

The Cowboy was cranky, I was cranky, the dog was cranky, but the yearlings were oblivious. To say that it was cold would be a huge understatement. We were now working in a full-on blizzard. Another failed attempt led to me getting a butt chewing for not being in the right place at the right time. Ladies, if you've ever worked with your hubby and any type of bovine, you know exactly what I mean. They forget that you're the one that cooks them dinner and you instantly become a "hand". I haven't heard of a ranch wife yet that hasn't screamed across sorting pens or pastures at her husband. Then at the end of the day, all is well again, no hard feelings...well, most of the time.

The issue at hand was this: I wasn't where I was supposed to be because I wouldn't lope my horse to get there. Well, you see, I didn't know where "there" was. I would have loved to get my horse "there" but "there" changed every other minute and I didn't know what "there" looked like in the first place! This was the source of a whole bunch of yelling from both parties. It didn't help that we were so far away from each other and the wind was blowing snow sideways. He thought it would be a good idea to come over and give me a lesson on getting my horse into a lope. This consisted of smacking my horse on the rump while telling me to get my horse moving. Now, I've had this horse longer than I've had that Cowboy. Guess where my loyalties were? I also didn't like being treated like a five-year-old. So I warned him. He did it again. I warned him and told him it was the last time. He did it again. I said, "You want to see me lope my horse? Watch this...." I loped straight home, flying the bird and my flag of self-righteous indignation held high.

I unsaddled my horse, put him away, and went into the house. I watched the rest of the scene through my kitchen window. It took the Cowboy a while to figure out what to do. We were, remember, on a deadline. So he called up a friend for some help. Our friend came to the Cowboy's rescue and together they finally got everyone gathered, sorted and shipped. The conversation over supper was short and sweet. "Sorry for yelling." Forgiveness was of course given. At least he knows, when I say I'm done, I mean it. That was the first and only time I've quit him...so far. We both learned lessons that day. The Cowboy learned that the wife will quit you if you go too far. I learned that "there" is a mysterious place when it involves yearlings.

Laugh Lesson:

When my daughter was almost two years old, I momentarily lost track of her. As is normal for toddlers, I found her with a handful of various treasures and a mouthful of random things. Most were edible, some not so much. Where kids find these things is a mystery that must be revealed in a toddler handbook that mothers were never meant to read. It did, however, remind me of a trip we took to the sale barn with Ray to buy calves to replace those yearlings we had just sold.

It was early winter and the weather was crisp to say the least. We started the trip with a stop at the gas station and Ray proclaimed his love for hot chocolate. With heated beverage in hand and truck back on the road, he began to tell us stories. He was born in 1907 so he had a few stored up. He'd lived in this valley all his life so he knew every family that lived in the now-abandoned homesteads. There was a name and a story for every fence line that existed, both now and years gone by.

I sat in the backseat with a notepad and pen, scribbling down the tellings of an old man. "There was a guy named Tom that lived just over there, up that draw a bit, and he had dealings with the Indians of the area. But he was crooked and they found out. They didn't like that much. We never saw him again, not that anyone missed him. He smelled so bad. I guess they did the rest of us a favor anyway."

The stories went on and on without a seam in between to hold them together. We passed a certain area that no one would take much notice of, except Ray. He said that he lost a good rope there one time. That was it, that's all he said. It was like he was waiting to be asked for further information. So the

Cowboy asked how it happened. A smile crossed Ray's face and he began to explain.

Ray and his younger brother Louis were on their way to their uncle's house some 50 miles away. They rarely got time away from the ranch so they took the chance to visit and go fishing. They were about 16 and 14 (he thought), and riding horseback. It was either ride or drive a team with the buckboard wagon. He was so proud of a new rope he'd just bought for $2.50. As they were riding, they were "Damn near run over by one of those Model Ts."

After some time of riding, they came upon that same Model T. It had slid off the road and was stuck in the mud. He said he thought about riding on but they decided to stop and help. The only thing they had to get this "contraption" out of the mud was Ray's brand new rope. After much struggling and tugging, they were able to free the car from the mud, courtesy of a two-horsepower effort. In the process, just as they thought they were in the clear, the rope broke.

Ray was "hopping mad". At first the guy they helped out wasn't even going to "help" them out. No reward or anything. Not even much of a thank you was offered. Then Ray began to tell the man about his new but now broken rope. I guess Ray made the guy feel guilty enough about it. The man said, "I can't give you much but this is all I have". It was a $2.50 reward. It was enough to buy a new rope. Ray, being the 16-year-old businessman he was, hoped for more but was satisfied. Louis was a little bent out of shape since he didn't get a "cut" but such is life for a younger brother. The stories continued all the way to the sale barn.

It was dark when we were done at the sale barn and headed for home. The trailer was a few thousand pounds heavier and Ray was happy with his new calves. Now we only had about 250 more to find. Ray didn't have near as many stories on the way home, probably due to the fact of not being able to see the landmarks in the dark. We picked up some fast food to take with us on the road because Ray never turned down food. You could always tell when Ray was eating. The three or four teeth that he had left were a little less than efficient so there was a bunch of chewing that had to be done. With this chewing action, his jaw would creak, grind, and crunch all at the same time. I guess when you're almost 100 years old, even your jaw gets tired of working.

WE WERE HALFWAY HOME AND IT HAD BEEN ABOUT 45 minutes since we were all done eating. Then we heard that same creak, grind, and crunch noise. Ray was chewing something but it didn't sound right. It sounded like he was chewing on a rock and any minute he was going to spit out his remaining teeth. I asked the Cowboy what Ray was eating because Ray could never hear a word I said. The Cowboy asked him what he was eating and it went a little something like this...

"What are you eating, Ray?"

"Piece of cheese." *Creak.*

"Where did you get a piece of cheese, Ray?"

"My coat pocket." *Grind.*

--What the? Laughter from the back seat--

"When was the last time you wore that coat?"

"Oh 'bout last fall when I went to buy calves." *Crunch.*

"You sure that cheese is still good? It is a year old."

"Oh, it's a little dry but still tastes alright. I guess you'll know if I'm dead in the morning."

The crunching went on for another 20 minutes till he finally had that cheese whipped. The laughter still continues when we think of Ray and that ride to the sale barn. I guess a two-year old isn't the only one that lives life dangerously and eats random things.

Hard Lesson:

A famous saying that I've heard from many different ranchers is that sometimes a calf is just born looking for a place to die. I just didn't believe that could be true. It didn't take long for me to understand exactly what they were talking about and we hadn't even come close to calving season yet. I had a lot to learn about life and death on the ranch.

The semi-truck finally pulled up with the last load of calves. Ray had bought close to 300 head to feed through the winter and then sell as yearlings in addition to the 200 or so home-raised calves. We didn't have to take them too far on horseback, thank goodness. We soon got all the little buggers settled into their new home.

45

It was only a few days until the first ones started coming down sick. The boss didn't believe in using medicine all that much so it took some convincing to get the okay to doctor these calves. Finally, with needles and brown med bottles in hand, we went to doctoring. We had already cut out the sick ones from the rest of the herd and brought them up to the corrals. One by one they went through the squeeze chute and got a couple pokes. We kept at the dosages and bringing in sick calves for a few more days. Some bounced back right away, some took longer, and some didn't at all.

There was a white steer that hadn't been doing so hot. He was the worst off. We gave him everything we could, the most we could, and the strongest stuff we could. It was like watching him take one step forward and then two backwards. Just when we thought to put him out of his misery, he'd bounce back for a day. This went on for a few days until I guess he gave up. The Cowboy and I were in the corrals letting the newly recovered calves out. We checked on that steer for about the third time that morning when it was obvious he was trying to kick the bucket. I started to tear up and said there had to be something else we could do for him. Cowboy told me he was past any help and sent me to go get the tractor.

So I somberly walked to get the tractor, for what I didn't know. I just assumed that my dear loving husband had my delicate sensibilities at mind and didn't want me to watch this steer die. Well, the Cowboy had things in mind, just not anything having to do with delicate sensibilities. The fact of the matter was this almost dead steer couldn't stay in the corrals after he stopped breathing. This is where the tractor came into play. As it would turn out, the only way to dispose of anything weighing 650 pounds is with a tractor.

I pulled up into the corrals and was relieved to know that by taking my sweet time in getting back I'd missed the fateful end of the steer. I was however crying a bit because I'd never seen an animal die, especially one who we'd fought so hard to keep alive. I get out of the tractor and Cowboy explained to me how we were to get the steer in position for disposal….he told me to grab a leg and roll him over. Well, I had started to compose myself by this point and realized that there was a job to do so I had to put on my big-girl pants and get it done. I walked over to the steer and broke out in hysterics.

I was sobbing so hard I couldn't even catch my breath! You know what I mean, crying sooo hard that catching your breath is kind of like a hiccup/ hyperventilating episode. Cowboy thought something was wrong and bailed out of the tractor. I had to yell over the noise of the tractor….

"*He's*... (breath, breath)…*Looking*... (breath, breath)… *At*...(breath, breath)…*ME!!!*" Sob, sob, breath, sob. "*Close*... (sob)… *His*... (sob)… *EYES!!!*"

Well, needless to say, the Cowboy got a swift punch in the arm for laughing at me. It took me a little longer to see the humor in the story.

There was something else I still had to learn. The

Cowboy then showed me the easiest way to tie an animal's feet so you can pick them up with the tractor. It wasn't a skill I wanted to learn but a necessary one all the same. You have to know how to care for an animal from birth to death, no matter how it comes about. I've also learned that's just the way it is on a ranch. You can't spend too much time crying over one that dies when you have hundreds more to try and keep alive. You can have life and death in almost the same minute.

2

SNOW

The snow crunched under my feet with every step I took. The house seemed so far away. It was pitch black dark and I wasn't sure what was better; breaking the trail or following my Cowboy. My stride was shorter than his anyway so I might as well break it to fit me. I was too afraid of coming up on some animal to actually ask for the lead. So I took the risk of some crazed carnivore coming up behind me and continued to follow my husband with a fistful of his coattails for good measure.

There was so much snow we had to park our truck at the road and walk up the driveway to our house. A half of a mile doesn't seem like much until you throw in two big hills and 14 feet of snow. A few times we took the "short cut" which consisted of parking in the usual spot, walking down the mostly plowed road, walking over the hardened snow that concealed the highway fence underneath and finally up the huge hill. Some days it was worth it, most days not.

It was some time in November that a profound statement was made to me. I huffed and puffed once again behind my then fiancé. The coyotes were sounding off somewhere down the valley. Their calls rose up to my ears and gave me a chill down my spine. I made my mumbles and grumbles loud enough for the valley to hear, partly to complain, partly to reassure myself that I wouldn't be attacked by a carnivore if I sounded scary enough. My fearless leader stopped, turned around and grabbed my hand. "Just think of all the stories we will have to tell our children."

I would be able to tell my children about how I trained a sled dog. After a few trips up that driveway carrying the groceries, I looked at my faithful dog at my side and a light bulb went off. I put my cow dog, Dally Mae, to work. I took an old martingale which is used for training horses and rigged up a harness. Once I attached a rein to both Dally's harness and an empty laundry basket, we were on our way. She wasn't thrilled about the basket following her but she didn't want to be left behind either. It was a long winter so she got lots of practice. I never did trust her with the eggs but she did settle into her new role of chief transporter of canned goods and toilet paper quite well.

I never did have a comment on the Cowboy's statement until much later that winter. It was sometime in February that I replied, "Seriously, do we have enough stories yet?" We were far from done making stories and I'm all the better for it.

Before I met the Cowboy, I did have to do some things on my own. He doesn't always believe that this is possible but, once upon a time, I was a very independent woman. I moved across the country, away from all family, just to chase a dream. Once that dream landed in my lap, I had to adjust and overcome to keep a hold of it. This included many things and horse trailers were just one of them. I know, doesn't seem very in-depth but it's a huge challenge that many do not overcome.

I learned to hook up my trailer by myself with no help backing up at all. I'm not going to reveal how many attempts this took because it's irrelevant, in my opinion. I've stuck to my guns this long, why give in now? Anyway, not only could I hook up my bumper pull trailer, I could drive with it too. My first scary moment came when I was driving over Togwotee Pass. I was returning to college from working in Jackson Hole, along with my roommate Joelle. We were in similar classes, we lived together, and she got me the job taking out trail riders in Jackson Hole. The season was now over so we loaded up her horse Lil and my Tango and away we went. We didn't have any major problems other than crawling up at like 25-mph because my truck was a little gutless until we were on the way down into Dubois (pronounced 'doo-boys' and don't let anyone tell you any different because you'll get laughed at if you actually go there and say it like a French person). The trailer got to shaking and squirreling around. I knew that was usual for a bumper pull trailer and just adjusted and went on. Whew! I always get so worried with horses in a trailer. I suppose it's good though; it makes you aware of what you're doing. That was my only close call with a horse trailer but here are those familiar words; that is, until I met the Cowboy.

When we first arrived at the ranch, we had left our horses at my parents' house. We did this so we could go around the fence and check the condition of the grass in the pastures. After a couple weeks of settling in and checking things out, we were setting out to collect our "herd". We only had two horses at the time, Tango and Star. So away we went over Monarch Pass and through the canyon along the Arkansas River. It was a little snowy over the pass but it wasn't anything major since it wasn't even sticking to the ground.

We had the ranch trailer hooked on; it was a gooseneck stock trailer, nothing fancy but it was light and pulled really well. We arrived at my parents' house, had a bite to eat, and made a quick shopping trip to gear up for winter. This included my first pair of coveralls and a wool "old man rancher hat" as I now affectionately call them. I swore I'd never be caught dead in one but I would learn later that they've been around for 100 years for a reason.

With the shopping trip over, we quickly loaded up the horses and were off again for the two-hour drive home. By the time we came through Salida, the halfway point just before the Pass, it was an "oh, crap" moment. There were a few inches of snow on the ground. If you've ever lived near the mountains, you know, if there's a little snow at the bottom, there's a bunch of snow at the top. That's just where we had to go, up and over. The closer we got to the start of the Pass, the more semi-trucks were pulled over putting chains on. I just kept saying over and over, "This can't be good."

Unlike my limited experience, I knew the Cowboy had been in similar situations and would know what to do. I had to keep telling myself that to stay calm. All the signs were flashing "four-wheel drive vehicles only" and "chain law in effect". We were already in four-wheel drive when we came to a pull out spot; it was a "last chance to get your chains on" place. So we parked and went to work getting the chains on. When we got back onto the road, I already had a knot in the pit of my stomach. We could only see about 20 feet in front of us. The rhythm of the noisy chains wasn't helping my nerves at all. I tried to stay really quiet so as to let the Cowboy focus on the task at hand. Soon I was doing what you've come to expect me to do....I was crying. A terrible movie kept playing in my head of a jackknifed gray Dodge truck with horse trailer attached laying on its side and my horses in the back needing to be shot from having all four legs broken. Yes, worrywart I am, but that wasn't the worst scenario I could think of. If I could have seen the edge, a sheer drop-off of however many thousands of feet, I probably would have been playing the movie of all our deaths. Even though I knew it was there, lucky for me, I couldn't see it so the first movie was playing.

We knew we were getting close to the top, but there was also more than a foot of snow on the ground so it was hard to tell exactly how close. A semi-truck with apparently more guts than us came along and passed us and blew his horn. Weird, but whatever; if he wanted to rush to his death, he was welcome to it! Then we got to looking around and we weren't exactly on the road. I can't even begin to express the wave of panic that came over me. I'd never truly hyperventilated in my life...until that moment. I had to roll down the window for some fresh air since there wasn't a paper bag in sight, and I was too afraid to put my head between my knees and to take my eyes off the road or what should have been the road! So at this point, I'm not making it very easy for the Cowboy to concentrate on not killing us. Now he's worried about his hysterical wife in the passenger seat because it wasn't enough to worry about the trailer staying straight, not sliding backwards, the foot and a half of snow, not being able to see, and - oh yeah - getting back on the road. I was finally able to breathe a quick sigh of relief when we reached the summit. Then I remembered we had to go back down. The Cowboy shifted low and away we went. Going down wasn't near the out-of-breath experience that going up was.

When we were at the bottom and back on good roads, the Cowboy finally acknowledged my presence. Ignoring me was his best way to keep focused. He said, "See? Safe and sound. No reason to cry." He is a man of few words but when he does speak, he just has to make it count. Obviously he had a different movie playing in his head than I did.

THE SNOW ON MONARCH PASS WAS JUST THE FIRST OF the snow experiences I'd have while on that first ranch. We soon learned that Ray loved to drive around the ranch and the winter months were no different. We made roads through the pastures to some of his favorite spots. To anyone else, it might have seemed like a waste of time but to keep up the spirits of an old man, it was worth it. Occasionally he would sneak off the ranch and drive towards town. Ray had an agreement with the city that they could use one of his pastures during the winter for snow dumping. When he'd randomly disappear, we would find him in that pasture counting the dump trucks of snow. We learned that this was how an old man keeps track of how much snow falls in town as opposed to out on the ranch. Not exactly scientific but entertaining all the same.

Very rarely did we get a day off since there wasn't anyone else to look after the ranch but, mainly, to look after Ray. One day after we fed the cows, we took off for a date. The Cowboy knew once calving season started there would be no days off for quite a long time so we took advantage of the time while we had it. We gave Ray instructions to stay on the driveway or, better yet, just stay inside his house and not go anywhere else because of the fresh snow from the night before.

When we came home from our date of dinner and a movie, we found Ray's truck stuck in the snow. It was exactly where we told him not to go. We quickly went into panic mode because we couldn't see him in the truck. He couldn't walk without his walker so we thought the worst. Did he try to walk to the house and freeze to death in a snowdrift? Did he finally figure out how to use his cell phone, call for help, and was now half dead in the hospital?

Upon closer inspection, he was in fact still in the truck but slumped over in the seat. Great. He never wore a coat; he instead relied upon the truck's heater. The Cowboy opened the truck door fully expecting to find a half frozen 97-year-old man popsicle. Ray jumped to life, scaring the Cowboy, and then acted a little grumpy at being woken up from his nap. As was the norm for Ray, he had a simple yet profound statement to sum up the whole evening to go with his grin. "You were right. The snow is deep."

After working for Ray, I learned to expect the unexpected. Several years after that first tough winter, I had an unexpected visitor. A very strange one, to say the least.

We lived about 60 miles from the nearest town so we weren't exactly on the way to anywhere. Most of those miles were dirt roads and our driveway alone was over a mile long, uphill. Needless to say we didn't get much company. Winter time we got even less.

For all those reasons, in addition to a two-day blizzard we were having, I was very surprised to hear a knock on my door. The roads hadn't been plowed since the blizzard started and there wasn't much hope of them being done any time soon. The plow operator was on a volunteer basis so if he didn't need to get out and go to town, you weren't getting out either. The Cowboy was still working on the other side of the 90,000 +/- acre ranch so I wasn't expecting him back any time soon. I happened to be cooking supper when I went to answer the door.

I wasn't sure if I should be afraid or full of pity for the young man that stood before me. He was dressed in a light jacket, dress pants, and dress shoes. The first thought that went through my head was he's one dedicated Jehovah's Witness! The second thought was that he must have missed the "it's winter in Wyoming" memo. I invited him in to warm up. I then got on the mountain "telephone" which was really a CB radio for the people on the mountain to communicate and relay messages. Most of us didn't have phone lines but the few that did have them never worked through the winter months anyway. No, there wasn't cell reception there either. I sent out a call for anyone seeing the Cowboy to send him home; there was someone that needed help. This was mainly to alert everyone that I was home alone with a stranger and that it was yet to be determined if he was a serial killer or not.

With the whole mountain on alert, I laid down my daughter for a nap, made sure the shotgun was handy, and went back to cooking. While I finished supper, I learned the young man's story. He had been snowed in for a couple of days at the nearby church camp. He was to be the new caretaker when on his way up he got his vehicle stuck. He wasn't that far from the camp so he walked the rest of the way. After a couple days at the camp, he started to run low on food. Then he rode a dirt bike, with no headlight, several miles till he saw a house with a light on.

I did what any ranch wife would do. I filled his belly full of elk steak, mashed potatoes, veggies and cake. Then I opened my cupboards to stock him with essentials to carry him through until he could replenish his own stocks. Then the Cowboy came home. He was just in time to fill his own belly and turn around and give the young man a ride back to his cabin after fitting him with an old pair of snow boots. He gave the Cowboy a tie in trade. We never heard from him again.

I THINK IT'S SAFE TO SAY THAT THE FIRST YEAR ON A ranch was a bit of a culture shock for me. The freezing temps, feeding cows, four feet of snow, and rancher-tan face with a white forehead had taken its toll on my psyche. I looked like a short chubby boy every day of that winter. I even tromped around our local watering hole in snow boots and coveralls on a Friday night. I've never been a "wear make-up every day" kind of girl but, seriously, I was beginning to think I'd forget how to put it on in the first place.

Then it was February. I started to protest. I warned my husband that our first Valentine's Day as a married couple was not going to involve coveralls and old man rancher hats! We still had to feed of course, but the evening was to be romantic. A couple of days before the big event, I drug the Cowboy into town to find some shoes. We went in and out of several stores in the small town but found nothing to match my outfit that I'd been saving for just such an occasion.

Then finally in the thrift store, I found them! A pair of silver high heels, very, very high, that had crisscross straps over the toes and one delicate strap around the ankle. Terribly inappropriate shoes for February in Gunnison, Colorado, not to mention the ranch. However, they were also terribly cute, sexy and wonderfully girlie. They were just what I needed to give me a boost in the middle of a long winter and an even longer ranch experience; little did I know the worst calving season ever lay ahead of me.

The 14th was finally here. Everything was fed and taken care of. I was in the bathroom for the longest time trying to remember how to apply make-up, curl my hair, and otherwise appear womanly. I had to wear my snow boots to the truck. I waited to strap on the silver girl shoes once we were on pavement, out of fear of getting stuck and having to get out and shovel snow or push the truck.

We stopped at the local watering hole since our dinner reservations weren't until later. Several of our friends were doing the same. I put my coat down next to the Cowboy and headed for the ladies room. While I was gone, the Cowboy got quite the earful. He was grilled by everyone around him. "Where's your wife?" "What do you think you're doing, out with another woman?" "I can't believe you'd do something like this!"

When I came back, everyone was normal. The Cowboy told me to talk or do something to convince everyone that I was in fact his wife. I wasn't sure if this was to be taken as a compliment or not. Was I so ugly before as a short chubby boy clad in Carharts? At least I knew that the whole town would stand up for me if the Cowboy tried anything funny! HA! I guess the girl shoes had served their purpose. I in fact looked like a girl; so much so, that I was unrecognizable.

We went on to our reservations after everyone had a good laugh at the wife mix-up. Dinner was wonderful and we still talk about the seven-layer chocolate cake. My toes were half frozen and bright red by the time we got home. The Cowboy had to help me to the door since I didn't feel like putting on my snow boots just to go from the truck to our front door. I kept sinking in the snow. It didn't matter though; they were cute and made me feel like a girl. That was just what I needed on a ranch that was covered in four feet of snow.

3

FEEDING

Y ou can learn many things from the back of a hay wagon. I've learned so many things over the years. I've also thought about many things while pitching hay to cows. I even wrote a song that will never be heard by anyone, ever.

I think more people should feed cows with square bales. Not the little ones, that's just crazy talk. I know all about feeding 10 tons per day of small squares for a month straight. The feeding isn't the tough part; it's the loading and the miles and miles of baling twine you have to deal with. Although, now that I think about it, I lost some weight and had some pretty nice guns; biceps in case you were wondering. Maybe those small squares weren't so bad...

As I've said before, during my first ranch experience, I pitched hay while the Cowboy drove. I was too afraid of getting the tractor stuck or going the wrong way where there wasn't a crossing. Besides, I had coffee to drink and cigarettes to smoke; I couldn't be bothered with driving. So I rode on the back, sitting on the hay, surrounded by dogs and had the view of a lifetime. I got to know "my" cows and then eventually their calves from the back of the wagon. I also solved many of the world's problems but the solutions involved too much common sense to be plausible.

I talk to myself constantly while I'm feeding. I'm terrible. Even when there are other people around to talk to, I still catch myself talking to myself. That has to be like a crazy person double negative or something; catching yourself talking to yourself.

It used to be just the Cowboy and me on the feeding crew. However, we soon had a new recruit coming up through the ranks: our daughter. When she was just two years old, she loved to drive. We would put the truck in four-wheel drive and in low gear so the truck would creep along; then we would bail out and jump on the feed wagon. Our new driver would put her blue bear that she refused to go anywhere without either on the dash so "he can watch cows, Momma" or under her arm so "Boo dive Nay-nay, Momma". She takes her job very seriously, too...well, most of the time. When she's not playing in the front seat or turning on the radio, she does a very good old lady farmer drive. You know; creeping along, one arm out the window, little hands on a giant steering wheel, and sitting on her feet so she can see out the window. When you yell for her to start turn-ing, you never know which way she's going to go but afterwards she does ask, "Good, Daddy? Good, Momma?"

One time when we returned to the truck after feeding, we found an extra proud driver. While standing on the seat, she proclaimed, "Nay-nay row-whoa-wee-whoa!" Even with all my motherly translation skills, I could not for the life of me decipher this toddler's gibberish. I thought maybe if she said it a couple more times, I could begin to make out enough to guess at the rest. No luck. We did the usual ignorant parent "uh-huh" to dismiss the whole ordeal.

Three whole days went by and every time it was the same when we returned to the truck from feeding. "Nay-nay row-whoa-wee-whoa!" Sometimes she'd even say it slower and louder like a silly American tourist in a foreign country trying to get a point across to a clueless non-English speaking person. Finally I said the magic words "show me". Then a very frustrated two-year-old cranked and cranked and rolled down the window. With a huge "duh" face she again proclaimed, "Nay-nay row-whoa-wee-whoa!" Finally I exclaimed, "Nay-nay roll down window!" Oh the things you learn while feeding cows.

OVER THE YEARS I'VE COME UP WITH MY OWN SYSTEM for feeding from a wagon. It drives my husband crazy but it works for me. I've also come up with a few pointers for both the person doing the feeding and the person doing the driving. Well, six pointers to be exact.

1. When the wagon is empty, just stay on the wagon. You have to close the gates anyway. It's too much effort to climb all the way back in the truck or tractor. Save your energy. Remember, it's still early.

2. When you ride on an empty wagon, sit to the front. There's a minefield of frozen cow turds out there and if you hit them while sitting on the back, you'll get ejected. Abruptly. Swiftly. Face in a snow bank. Or worse, you'll land back on the rock-hard boards of the wagon. Trust me on this one, live and learn.

3. If you're the one driving, don't try to be helpful. Don't stop and start 50,000 times just because a flake of hay didn't hit the ground. Just drive. Try to avoid the minefields. That's all I ask of you.

4. If there's a missing board on the hay wagon that you've been stepping around all winter because you know it's there, don't assume anyone else knows it's there. While this does make for a good laugh for you, it doesn't always translate well to the other person. So tell them ahead of time. In my case, it was my dear Cowboy that didn't listen to me when I told him about it in the first place so I did laugh. Very loudly. For a long time.

5. Don't worry if it takes you a while;

eventually you'll get your "wagon" legs. You'll start off looking like a cross between a drunken sailor and a toddler that can't stay upright but have no fear, you'll get there. Soon you'll be jumping around that hay like a barn cat, all while the wagon is moving. Only when your husband stomps on the breaks and then yells, "Oops, sorry" will you be thrown off the wagon. It's okay though because then you're already on the ground and you can get to the truck door faster before he locks it for fear of his life. It's better if you don't ask how I know this.

6. When you're sitting on top of a few tons of hay while it lumbers along, just breathe. Listen to the crunch of the snow, the creaks and squeaks of the wagon, and the livestock as they come to greet you. Watch the hawk soaring high above you, the calves jump and play at the back of the herd, and the sway of the wagon that ambles along like an eight-month pregnant woman. Remember all these wonderful things because at some point it will be below zero and snowing sideways and something has to get you through that day!

I thought I'd never make it through that first winter. I was nowhere near in shape for pitching hay every morning. I had nowhere near enough anti-

freeze in my veins to deal with -30 degree temps. I
didn't think I had anywhere near enough grit to deal
with ranch life. Turns out you don't come up with
enough grit to stay on a ranch all in one day, lucky
for me.

4

PREPARATIONS

On a ranch you are always preparing for one thing or another. Normally when you hold a paycheck in your hand, it represents the last couple weeks of your life. When you are a part of a ranch that paycheck comes once a year and it represents the previous year and a half of your blood, sweat and tears. I understand all this now but at the time it was a very foreign concept to prepare so far in advance. This was especially true when we were attending a bull sale in February before we were even calving.

The boss, Ray, couldn't hear worth beans but he was sharp as a tack. He read the Denver Post every day along with an assortment of other newspapers and agriculture magazines. He would never watch his 40" TV but he could tell you all the stats on every player of the Denver Broncos. He saw a flyer for a bull sale and said he'd like to go since we were in need of another bull. When the time came, we hooked up a trailer, loaded up Ray, and away we went.

While on the two-hour drive to the sale, the Cowboy asked him what his favorite type of bull was. Ray responded, "Black Angus is my favorite as long as they're good looking and produce well." The Cowboy's response was, "If Angus is your favorite, why are we going to a Charolais bull sale?" Charolais is a breed of solid white cattle. Ray just chuckled like he always did, showing all three of his teeth, and shrugged his shoulders. That was Ray, one giant walker-using shuffle-walking contradiction. He prided himself on many things, one of which was that it took him 30 years to get kicked out of a grazing association. When the rest of the county was raising Herefords, he brought in an Angus bull.

You see, in a grazing association, everyone pools their cattle together on thousands of acres. Inevitably the cattle end up mixing together. This also happens to be right during prime breeding season. So if everyone has the same type of cows and bulls, there isn't a problem. These grazing associations even go so far as to buy community bulls so everyone ends up with the same type of calf crop. When Ray brought in a bull of a different breed and quite literally a different color, the rest of the ranchers weren't very happy when they ended up with a crossbred calf. Ray was just mischievous like that and chuckled the whole time.

We had a good day at the sale meeting new people, and seeing old friends and family. We were soon on our way home with a good-looking, snorty but ready for breeding season, two-year-old bull. As we were driving, a minivan passed us doing Mach 9 on the shoulder, throwing dirt and gravel everywhere. Then a truck soon passed us the correct way. It was very odd but we couldn't guess what the cause could be. About 20 miles later, there was a mob of county sheriffs and state troopers surrounding this minivan. We slowed but just went around until we saw the truck that had passed us and the driver was flagging us down. So the Cowboy pulled over. Ray asked what the trouble was and Cowboy told him he'd go check it out. So here we sat, Ray and I. He could never hear me even if I shouted. To make things worse, that bull was getting a little mad and started banging things around, rocking the truck every now and then.

Ray looked in the side mirrors. "I wonder what the hold-up is." Then he looked back at me with a grin. "Do you think they'll check us for marijuana?"

"WHAT?!?" I think he heard me that time. I tried yelling loud enough and reassure him they weren't going to search the truck. He replied, "Well, I got searched one time when my hired hand was driving me to the grocery store. They had a hard time getting me out of my pickup and I don't want to get out again." I assured him there was no reason for any of that and maybe it was a good thing he didn't have that particular hired man anymore.

A couple more minutes went by until Ray blurted out with a straight face, "I think we can outrun them." I laughed so hard I could barely say, "*How can we outrun them with a truck, trailer and a 2,000 pound bull?"* With a spark in his eye but still no smile on his face, he told me his plan. "You see, I think you can sneak back there without them noticing. Then you can swing that trailer door open. That bull's just wild enough he might take a few of them out and the others will be too busy running from him. Then you can come back, get in, and we'll make a break for it." Seriously, I have no idea how a 97-year-old man would come up with this. He didn't even watch TV. I still couldn't tell if he was serious or not. *"I guess so, Ray, but what about my husband?"* "Ahhh, he'll be fine. We'll get him later."

When all was said and done, the Cowboy just had to give a statement about the driver of the minivan and how he was recklessly driving. Come to find out, the vehicle was stolen. The truck that was following it just didn't want to lose sight of it until there was enough reception to call the authorities.

When the Cowboy returned I told him about Ray's escape plan. It was quite a surprise for the Cowboy to learn that he was going to be left behind. When he asked Ray why, Ray simply said, "Awe, I knew you could walk back to the ranch if you had to. Maybe you could have ridden that bull home." Finally, he gave a smile, showing all three teeth and a soft chuckle of a mischievous old rancher.

WHEN WE FINALLY RETURNED HOME, IT WAS ALMOST dark. The Cowboy backed the trailer up to the corrals while I guided him back to just the perfect spot. Meanwhile, we were being carefully watched by a cow that we called "Big Momma". We had brought her to the corrals for fear of an early calving due to a big belly and full bag of milk. She was huge to start off with weighing in at about 1700 pounds compared to the rest of the girls that averaged about 1200 or less. I can't even tell you how many times I would mistake her for one of the bulls. She outweighed the rest but was also about a foot taller. To her credit, she was laid back. She never went anywhere in too much of a hurry, never pushed her weight around with the other cows, and was never "snorty" or aggressive with any two-legged critter either. Nevertheless, she stood in the neighboring pen watching us unload this very wound-up young bull.

Right about here is when time started to slow down but not long enough for a person to actually stop the events that were about to unfold. Well, I take that back. A different person might have been able to but THIS person did nothing. It was almost completely dark when I watched the pure white bull jump out of the trailer as if his life depended upon it. I then watched as a black as night Big Momma headed straight for the opposite end of her corral. She was like a freight train gathering speed at a dead run for the four-board, almost six-foot high fence. There was no way she could get her 1700 pounds airborne to go over that thing, I thought to myself.

Little did I know but she had no intention of going over anything. In that moment of time, she was like the Incredible Hulk. Boards came crashing down, the noise of which drowned out the idling diesel truck, splinters were flying all around, and there was now a six-foot hole in the corrals where there was once a six-foot fence. She was gone, out of sight into the dark night, to join the rest of the herd that didn't include scary white bulls.

The Cowboy came running around the truck and trailer to where I was. My heart melted a little at the thought of him being so concerned for my safety. Well, that was silly of me. He ran past me to survey the damage, looking for blood from the cow and also to wave away the white bull. In my silly heart-melting moment I didn't notice the bull had jumped the fence into the formerly occupied corral and was in hot pursuit of the recent jailbreak. Upon seeing the Cowboy, the bull stopped in his tracks and remained on the far side of the pen. I was then instructed to "stand in the hole".

This would be the moment when sheer panic came over me for the 50,000th time since I'd been on this ranch. While I strongly protested, whined and cussed at my husband, I still found myself standing in the giant hole, staring down an even bigger bull. I felt every single pound of my heart in my chest as the seconds crawled by until the Cowboy came back with a metal panel and some wire. I held the panel while he pointed the truck lights so we could actually see what we were doing.

The events of the day were almost too crazy to believe but we were both happy that it was finally at an end. Big Momma never did go back into the corrals; she calved just fine on her own and was almost the last cow to do so. The bull never really did settle down until we put him out with the other bulls which quickly put him in his low-ranking place. The corral fence was fixed the next day with new boards that stood out among the weathered ones like a huge black eye...black as the cow that put it there.

AFTER WE TURNED OUT THE BULL, IT WAS THEN TIME TO prepare the corrals for calving season. We did all the usual things: clean water tanks, place feeders and mineral tubs, and make fluffy beds of clean straw. All these luxuries weren't meant for the whole herd of course; just the sick, weak or those "in trouble" and needing help.

It was then time to start riding through the cows to look for "heavies", those mommas that were ready to calve any day now. We were going to bring them into the smaller pasture closer to the house so we could check on them easier. This would be my first attempt at sorting pregnant cows, or any other type of bovine for that matter, from the back of a horse.

The Cowboy and I went to catch our horses when I was informed that I should ride Mellow Yellow, as I called her. I put up a slight protest but I knew I wouldn't get anywhere. At the time, the best horse on the place was my old man Tango. The Cowboy said the he needed to ride him in case things got out of hand. I'm not the least bit afraid to say that I'm not always the most accomplished rider and getting on a new horse still makes me a little nervous.

My nerves were eased a little at the fact that she was 20-something years old at last count. She was always the last one to get anywhere. She was the last of a bloodline that came from Ray's mares when he was breeding with a government-owned stud for the US Calvary remounts. After the stud was taken away through a series of events - mainly the fact that Ray was racing him at the Cattleman's Days and won the big shebang and then ended up in the statewide papers - Ray kept his mares and continued the working cow horse and part-Thoroughbred bloodline.

Yellow was formerly known as "Pig" but I quickly changed it because she seemed a little bit daintier than that. The name Pig was given to her because she was about as big around as she was tall and she kind of snorted funny when you rode her. She did this partly out of protest and mostly because she was so out of shape. It was all a part of her strategy to get out of being rode.

We soon got the horses all saddled up and ready to go. As we were walking toward the gate, I had to constantly squeeze her with my legs - otherwise known as "pedaling" - just to keep up. Well, pedaling a bike would have been easier and faster than riding this horse. She was sooooo slow, slower than an old trail ride horse slow. A 97-year-old man in a truck stuck in first gear beat us to the gate, then picked up his newspaper and caught up on the goings on of an entire town before we got there.

We finally showed up to the task at hand and luckily spotted our cow right off. That morning we fed close to the gate so ideally the sorting would go easy. Cowboy told me to just stay a little ways off from the gate to make sure she didn't go past it while he was going to push her up the fence. In other words, I was supposed to just be Plan B, or a scarecrow. I was relieved since I didn't have to try and work this cow on a horse that I was sure might just have a heart attack and die with me still in the saddle. No problem, I had the easy job, or so I thought.

So I sit and watch as Cowboy eases this cow out of the herd without a fuss...why does he make that look so easy?? Yellow watches, too, but only by turning her head without moving a single foot which would take too much extra effort. Ray was watching, as always, from the other side of the gate in his truck. I picked up my reins a bit since the cow is now getting close to the gate but she sees the hole, so no worries. Then a thought crossed my mind: *What is she doing??*

That was about all I had time to think about. Before I could even speak, the cow was past the gate and looking Yellow square in the eyes. The cow started to take a step to the left so I moved my reins about two inches to the left.

Now, I'm not sure I really believe in out-of-body experiences. However, if I did, I think this moment would be about as close as I will ever come. I didn't have time to scream, cry, or even grab the saddle horn. Yellow was squatted down, with back feet set, and then she went to cutting this cow. I think you'd be very safe to assume that I've never ridden a cutting horse of any caliber. That cow moved to the left and Yellow slammed her front end to the left...and the right, then left and right again. Each time the cow even thought about moving, Yellow slammed the door of escape shut.

It was a delicate dance between a wanna-be escaping cow and a horse that knew not to let her. A horse that knew to watch every slight shift in the cow's weight, every slight movement of her head and then react accordingly. A horse that not only knew the steps to this dance but also knew the rhythm and every note of the music. A horse that needed neither instruction nor a rider to orchestrate it all.

Now, let's get back to THAT rider for a second. Cowboy told me later that she moved so fast it was like he was watching a cartoon. You know the ones where just before they fall they're suspended in the air until they realize what's below? Yup, that was me. Yellow ducked out from under me so fast, I lost both of my stirrups and was suspended in air for a second until she came right back underneath me like nothing ever happened. It was like that's what she planned all along. Take care of business with the cow and take care of me. Wait, speaking of plans...

I was set up. Now it was all making sense. Ray watching, the easy cow all of a sudden trying to make a break for it...see where this is going? It was true. My dear loving husband was the mastermind. He had talked to Ray earlier about Yellow and Ray told him, "Oh, she'll watch a cow pretty good" with that same evil grin we had come to know so well. I'm pretty sure that was the understatement of the year. So my wonderful husband, who likes to put me in situations that I can learn from or sometimes he can laugh at, set me up. He was the one who pushed the cow too hard to get her to square up with Yellow.

Meanwhile, the cow was through the gate, I was done screaming - even if it did no good after the fact it did make me feel better - my heart was still pounding, and my horse was freaking out. Yes, "Mellow" Yellow was freaking out. She was acting worse than a three-year-old fresh off of green grass! She was prancing and dancing all over the place, mad at me for taking her away from the cows. I couldn't get her to stand still and on the way back to the corrals, she wouldn't think of walking.

Ray asked us later, "You think she'll watch a cow?" with a huge grin on his face. It didn't take me too long to get over being set up like that. I knew if I ever had to hold a bunch of cows or sort something off, I wouldn't hesitate to catch ol' "Mellow" Yellow again because she truly loved her job and it made her feel young again. I would just make sure to hold on the next time.

SPRING

Life. It's happening all around. Most days it's as natural and easy as breathing. Some days it's as difficult as walking on water. Every day you get a reminder that it's not all about you. The life that springs up at our feet in green grass, that wags its tail as a happy lamb, that stumbles as a newborn calf, that pushes a sprout through the recently thawed ground is nurtured and never taken for granted.

As I'm shoulder deep in cow uterus, he whispers, "Is this the romantic ranch life you were looking for?" I had no words, but laughed later.

1

THE BABIES ARE COMING!

I've been through quite a few calving seasons by now but some of the most memorable things happened in my very first one. If it wasn't for the trials and tribulations of that first calving season, the subsequent ones would not have been so easy. I went from knowing nothing about anything and always resulting in a screaming match with my husband to a very quiet barn with everything going smoothly since we both knew our jobs and had done it so many times we barely even had to talk.

That barn door on the first ranch should have been a revolving one. In one day we had to pull seven calves. I finally gave up trying to get the baby goo off of me. I rinsed off with the almost freezing water from the trough and went on to the next like an old pro.

It might come as no surprise that my hands are smaller than the Cowboy's. Most of the time the size of his hands are to his advantage around the ranch since he's able to do many things that I can't. However, it might surprise you that sometimes small hands are very welcome, necessary even. This is especially true in the case of big calves and first time mommas, otherwise known as heifers.

The Cowboy and I made it through the first bunch of cows with no problems. I quickly figured out how to tell if the feet were in the right position instead of breech. This was a pretty big step for me since, up until this point, I'd never even seen a calf born. I would take my shift and ride through the cows then sit and watch birth after birth. Then along came time for the heifers to start calving. We soon learned that the previous manager didn't use a heifer bull; a bull that is chosen to breed with only the heifers because he throws low birth-weight calves to make it easier to give birth. The very first heifer to calve was my most memorable.

The Cowboy could tell she was having problems right off so we got her into the barn which, by the way, didn't have a chute or anything of the like. We had a small metal panel attached to the wall in a dark corner. Now at this point, I didn't know that it's much easier to get a cow to go through a chute or at least something with an opening. I guess it's the old "light at the end of the tunnel" kind of thing. If a cow doesn't see daylight or a way she thinks she can get out, chances are you're going to go round and round until you can convince her that there isn't a boogie man in the dark corner waiting to eat her.

So after a few turns of the dark barn she finally

went into this corner. We tied up the rope at the end of the panel to keep her from backing out. The calf had one toe already sticking out. Cowboy rolled up his sleeves and began feeling around in the cow's uterus for the other leg of the calf, otherwise known as "fishing". He had hopes that she might then be able to push on her own. No luck. I handed him the ob chains.

Now just to pause for a second, ob chains can vary in types. They are used to put on the calf's legs and pull either by hand or attached to a glorified come-along winch. The type of chains we had were the extra long dog collar choke chains so nothing got pinched on the calf or cow. I wasn't fully aware of the necessity of a "no pinch" factor until I saw the whole thing in action. I thought any old chain would do until I figured out where it all went. Then I understood and had all the sympathy in the world. As it would turn out, baling twine, belts or just some rope that was in the back of the truck will also do in a pinch. As any rancher will tell you, more than one calf has been pulled without veterinarian-grade ob chains.

As I'm watching him put on the first chain on the calf's leg, I'm standing ready to hand him the next....no such luck. He looks at me and says, "Your hands are smaller." I replied, "Yeah, so? What's your point?" I wasn't trying to be humorous; I really didn't get where he was going with this. He then quickly explained to me that the calf had a leg hung back too far for him to reach and if we didn't get it pulled soon, they might both die. Well that was enough to send me into hysterical crying and shouting, "I don't know how!"

I was then given a five-second instructional that went something like, "Stick your hand in, feel around, get the foot straightened out, get the chain on, man-up, do it now!" So after that, I was even worse. I screamed, "JUST GIVE ME A SECOND!" I then sounded like I was the one in labor; taking a few deep breaths, Lamaze style, to psych myself as I rolled up my sleeves and took off my rings. I'd heard horror stories of lost wedding bands and no we didn't have any gloves handy at that moment. 1...2...2 1/2 ....3! It's a good thing he told me to stick my "hand" in instead of what he really meant....my whole arm. So now I'm fishing for this missing leg and I can't even begin to describe to you the awful expression on my face. In no time I pull out the leg with chain on and all. Now I'm covered in baby-goo and the real work begins. Cowboy goes to pulling and I'm at the tail end of the cow signaling when she's pushing. We continued this for a few minutes until I caught an 85-pound calf and put him on the ground.

There I was, standing with a tear-streaked face in a dark 100+-year-old barn, looking down at the first calf that not only did I help bring into this world but the first that I touched inside a cow's womb, covered in baby calf-goo; thinking to myself that it didn't matter how I came to be here, just that I loved every second of it. And my small hands.

. . .

THE CHARMS OF DAYBREAK ON A RANCH HAVE SLOWLY converted me to become more of a morning person. When the Cowboy and I first met, I was known to sleep until noon; ah, the good old days before I had lives depending on me for their existence. And diaper changes. And pop tarts. I remember how hard the Cowboy had to try to get me out of bed after a long night of checking cows. With eyes still closed, I pointed to the window. "Do you see that? The sun isn't even up so why do I have to be?" I think it's been my credo since birth and I will probably defend it to the death, even if only in principle. I've been a hard convert, to say the least. At some point, I realized that some of the best and worst things happen in the mornings. The best would be coffee. The worst would be heifers calving. Both are reasons to get my lazy butt out of bed.

The Cowboy attempted to wake me up yet again but gave up and went outside to check cows without me. It seemed like we had just checked five minutes ago but it was really two hours. He came back in a hurry and said something about a heifer and come quick. I did just that with the frazzled and clumsy coordination of a hippo on land. I went out to see what was so urgent as I thought surely he was over-exaggerating just to get me out of bed. There she lay, paralyzed, calf mostly out and they were hip-locked. What the...? I'd never seen anything like it, not even in the cow books the Cowboy made me read. Basically, it's when a perfect storm happens. The hips of the calf rotate the wrong way and "lock" with the momma's hips so calf gets stuck and no amount of pushing from momma will help.

He had been watching her calve and she was doing just fine. She was a typical heifer and was getting up and laying down quite a bit, just unsure of what to do next. In all her up and down first-calf-heifer frenzy, the calf twisted just enough to lock those hips. Again the lack of a heifer bull didn't help matters at all.

The Cowboy quickly tells me what to do. We soon have her restrained since she was attempting to get up. She was paralyzed to a point but still dragging this poor calf along. My heart was breaking to see her try to get up and hearing the calf bawl at its less than normal entrance to this world. The Cowboy tried to push the calf backwards a bit but that wasn't working. The next recommended step is to roll a cow onto her back and pull the calf through her back legs toward her belly. I don't know about you but I'd never tried to roll a cow onto her back before. I don't think that this is what is meant by "cow-tipping" either. Well, if you ever randomly need to attempt this, I'd suggest you didn't. Just a word to the wise: Don't try to roll a cow onto her back with a calf hanging half out. I know, I know, that's what numerous books will tell you but I'd recommend skipping this last resort step and just call a vet.

So somewhere in the middle of all this, I did call the vet on my cell phone. He would be here ASAP. We were trying to pull the calf through her legs, only with the heifer on her side. We just didn't have the manpower to pull, try to rotate the calf, and keep her restrained in the middle of the pasture. So the vet came like a welcome superhero and away we went. So, now four people are involved in saving both heifer and calf. One to restrain, one to pull her leg to rotate her hips, one to pull and one to rotate the calf. See even the vet didn't try to roll her on her back! A couple of minutes later, baby BeeBee was born. Momma was still a little paralyzed and exhausted. BeeBee was swollen from the hips down and couldn't walk from the ordeal but was otherwise healthy.

The heifer never really came into milk despite all our efforts of milking and shots. I went to the barn every few hours and fed BeeBee a bottle. She was actually strong enough to start walking in no time. She sustained some nerve damage or lack of blood flow was the only thing we could figure since she couldn't pick up her back feet all the way. She would take a few steps just fine then break down in the fetlock joint, which is basically her ankle joint, and drag her hooves. As many ranchers before us have done, we made casts for her. The casts seemed to help. Progress was slow but she had all the heart in the world.

If you've never bottle-fed a calf long enough for them to call you "Mommy", you don't know what you're missing. Yes, it's a pain in the butt but it's so cute, too. She was a chocolate-latte colored, big doe-eyed, milk-sucking, slobbering ball of sheer cuteness. I made sure she was fat with milk and I'd play around the pen with her so she'd get a bit of exercise without straining anything. She was getting stronger and was now almost a month old.

She was doing so great and I was so proud of my first bottle calf. I went out one morning and she was looking a little "off". So I watched her and a few hours later I noticed her poo. She had Scours, a really bad flu for calves, with horrible diarrhea and severe dehydration that strikes very quickly. We doctored her right away so as to give her the best chance possible. The next few days were a roller coaster ride.

Then one morning we pulled up to the barn with bottle in hand and I started bawling. Cowboy couldn't figure out what was wrong with me. I said, "She's dead, she's dead I just know it." He couldn't even see her so he said, "No, let's go look." She always greeted me at the gate and I just knew by the way she was lying. I was devastated. I got back in the truck, still holding the bottle. We still had to feed the rest of the herd and I bawled all morning and even now, remembering her. I'd seen calves die before, even ones we fought to save, but this was just terrible. I made the Cowboy "take care" of her. I just couldn't.

It became a little less hard to wake me up after all that. It's kind of like picking your nose on a bumpy dirt road while riding in an old beat up ranch truck that the shocks went out on 100,000 miles ago. It's not easy, it takes some practice and skill, but you get used to it. I still had a ways to go but the Cowboy's words were finally sinking in and taking hold. "The livestock come first."

Mornings are no longer a foreign country to me.

While I still might not talk much for fear of chewing someone's head off, I've learned to like and dare say "enjoy" mornings. I enjoy the quietness of the ranch as the sun comes up, when you hear the birds singing and the occasional bawl of a calf. I enjoy the alone time with a cup of coffee. Most of all, I enjoy the mornings when I don't wake up to calving problems.

WHILE WE WERE OUT CHECKING THE PAIRS OF MOMMAS and babies one day, the Cowboy said something that has always stuck with me. "It's kinda like Easter egg hunting." If you catch them at just the right time of day, the whole nursery goes down for a nap. They curl up in a good hiding spot and take a snooze. It's then that they are the hardest to find which makes counting calves pretty interesting. I don't know if all cattlemen do this but, me being a worrywart, I was always counting.

My first calving season, my record book was a little more unique than others. Every time a calf hit the ground, I wrote down the date, sex of calf, and tag number of momma. Now this is what most people do; some will also add birth weights and ease of calving for the cow. I wasn't so concerned with that. My main priority was that they all had names. I still have that record book, many years later, and can recall almost every calf. There were a few that had earned their names more so than others, like Lucky. There was also Backwards, Oscar, Twist, Squeeze, Dumbo and Splash. Most of these were named due to obvious reasons. Baby Plop on the other hand you might not guess so well since most babies hit the ground with a bit of a "plop" anyway.

I was standing on my porch one day when I saw a cow making circles, laying down, getting back up, and then repeating the cycle. It was a sure sign she was getting ready to pop. She moved out of view behind one of the barns so I hopped on the four-wheeler and rode over closer to watch and make sure all was okay. I was a good distance away so as not to disturb her but still had a watchful eye through the binoculars. The Cowboy was just getting in from moving yearlings and was unsaddling. He came over and joined in the "watching".

She had just settled down and was doing a great job of pushing when she was….well, let's say, interrupted. You see, this whole time the 97-year-old boss man was driving around in his pickup like he did every day. His eyesight was failing but he still thought of himself as the ever-vigilant cattleman. I think he just liked to watch them calve as a break from the newspaper he read every day. He would bump into a cow every now and then, and how he didn't run over a calf, I'll never know.

We were watching her closely and she was doing just fine. In no time flat, she had front feet, head then shoulders out in about two pushes. The serenity of the birth was smashed by the roar of an engine. That Ford pickup came barreling through the pasture and around the corner of the barn. I wasn't sure if he was going to get that thing shut down in time! He stopped and laid on the horn. His front bumper was about a foot away from her tail end. I've never seen a cow get up that fast, let alone with a calf hanging half out. And I have never known a cow to be graceful at anything, much less to move with any type of fluidity in their body. Nevertheless, this cow became a bovine ballerina when she stood up and spun around to meet that bumper head on. Of course this was all while being honked at. The cow came to an abrupt stop but the calf kept going. Just imagine a 90-pound black calf flung from his momma's body with a terrible suction noise, then being spun around like the propeller of a helicopter with each leg pointing straight out, then landing a good ten feet away from momma. What an entrance!

I was both appalled and dying with laughter. We ran over to inspect the calf to find he was just fine and no worse for the wear. When we asked the boss man why on earth he did such a thing, he said, "I thought she was having problems and if I got her up the calf wouldn't be stuck." Well, I guess that's one way of getting a cow up. I could think of a few better ways though.

I THINK LIFE IS FUNNY SOMETIMES. WHEN I WAS growing up and even into adulthood, my family referred to me as the non-crier of the bunch. I'm the youngest of four girls so estrogen was thrown around with the Kleenex. I, however, wasn't always on board with the showing of emotion. I believe "stoic" or "ice queen" was mentioned a time or two. Maybe 12.

It's just a little ironic that this thing I call Ranch Life has brought out the tears in me. I think that the life and death struggle we as ranchers go through every day has something to do with it. It's also the fact that we entrust ourselves with the extreme responsibility of caring for other living beings. I think that's what makes ranch men quiet and realistic. In turn, the ranch women are extra caring and loving.

My first lambing season came after many calving seasons. While cows and sheep are very different animals, basic anatomy and birthing problems are very similar. So I dove in with both feet at the new ranch we were on and welcomed the challenge. I still had the help of the Cowboy of course, but I was confident enough to do the checking, bottle feedings, and even sheep-hooking by myself. I would go to the lambing barn, check the ewes, hook a back leg with a sheep crook, and take any inside that looked like they would lamb soon.

Within the first two weeks, I was knee deep in baby sheep! I watched the birth of twins and helped with a set of triplets. The second lamb was breech and had to be pulled. Once it was out of the way, the third lamb quite literally shot out making a grand entrance. This particular ewe would mother the two girls while she pushed the first-born boy away. So I was again a foster mom.

I would milk other ewes that only had a single lamb and then bottle-feed the bum lamb. For a long, drawn-out reason that doesn't much matter now, I named him Piss Willy. My then two-year-old daughter was in love with him, as was I. It's very hard to not fall in love with a baby lamb. They are so fuzzy and tiny that they just need to be hugged and kissed. Repeatedly.

I took this lamb all over with me since he didn't have a momma to keep him warm. Occasionally, I would take him home. My daughter would feed him from the NICU bottles we were given for her when she was born. Then the racing up and down the hallway would soon start. This was followed up by a nap in a lamb-sized nest on the floor made from her favorite blankets. Eventually, Piss Willy would have to be a real lamb but we had to find him a mom first. So we waited.

One morning when I was checking sheep, I found her. A ewe that had twins; one was alive and one was dead. My heart sank for a second but I had to get them into the barn before the live one got too cold. After a few struggles, she was safe and sound in the barn and the lamb was up and sucking, as they say.

Soon the Cowboy was there to help. I told him what happened and he said, "Let's go." I thought this meant go home for a cup of coffee before feeding cows. Silly me.

It meant, "Show me where the dead lamb is." I took him over to where the little one lay. At this point I was okay, no tears. Then the Cowboy pulled out his pocketknife. I knew this would happen when I found the little one dead; it meant that Piss Willy would have a real chance at having a mommy.

Two seconds after the click of the pocketknife, the Cowboy went to work skinning. I've seen many things skinned in my life due to the various hunting seasons. Seriously, this was so different. I didn't start crying until I had to help hold him. I lost it. I just started bawling! I was cussing everyone and their dog for letting this lamb die so I had to help skin it. I didn't care if Piss Willy was an orphan all his life at that point. I just cried and cried. I felt like a little kid. You know how a kid cries with no care about where the tears fall or how much the snot is running out of their nose? Yup, that was me, sitting on the half-frozen ground with my pajamas tucked in my boots in the middle of the sheep corrals.

I really needed some coffee. It would have to wait; we needed to take care of Piss Willy. His newly-fashioned coat was jet black in stark contrast to his own white fleece; an ever-present reminder of what had to happen for him to get a second chance. I picked him up and it fit him perfect. He went straight to sucking and his new momma didn't seem to mind. He only wore it for a couple days before I took it off and he was fully accepted by his new mom and sister.

This Ranch Life has taught me many things, one of which is to cry. Sometimes on the toughest of days, you just have to. Just remember that at some point you do have to wipe the tears away. When you do, there will be a new little miracle waiting to show you a thing or two. Then you can go get some coffee.

* * *

EVEN WHEN YOU'RE IN THE THICK OF CALVING OR lambing, Mother Nature gives you a glimmer of hope. This is usually in the form of signs of spring in between the snowstorms. Somewhere along the line, I've developed a theory. I think I noticed it long before I was on a ranch but it just grew stronger and stronger the closer I got to nature. I have no idea if it holds any merit - my husband still doesn't think so - but here it is: Watch the skunks. Profound, I know. Once you think that winter will never loosen its grip, look for the skunks. Warm weather is just around the corner if you start seeing these little stinkers out and about. The same goes for fall; the cold is coming when you see them, even if they are usually dead in the road.

The Cowboy and I were off to the stack yard to load up hay and feed cows yet again. We had made our rounds already checking cows for signs of calving and all was well. We had an old feed wagon pulled behind a tractor that was my "post". My faithful Dally May dog was always at my side for the bumpy ride.

In case you're wondering, yes, the Cowboy drove the heated tractor while I pitched off hay. Daily he would ask me if I wanted to drive but my dirty look told him no. You see, by the time I had a few cups of coffee, a bumpy ride to get to the hay, opened a few gates, pitched a few tons of hay to get some aggression out, and smoked a few cigs, I was ready for human contact but not a single minute before.

As we approached the stack yard, I saw it. The little Peppy Le Pew meandering around the stack. I "signaled" the Cowboy which translates into me jumping off the hay wagon and running alongside the still-moving tractor. He told me to get the dog so I threw Dally into the cab of the tractor. He then said he was going to get the gun and for me to follow it. What the...? FOLLOW a skunk? Now I'm thinking to myself....Self, exactly how close do you follow a skunk? Well, myself didn't follow very close at all! In fact, I let him get a pretty good head start.

So while I'm trying not to get sprayed by following too close, Cowboy comes tearing up on the four-wheeler, minus a dog, plus a 22 small-caliber rifle. Now normally we are 'live and let live' kind of people. If an animal isn't threatening the herd or us, we leave it alone. So now you're thinking, what about the innocent little skunk? Well, these innocent little skunks were heck to get rid of when they decided to nest in the crawlspace of my house! So we were too close to my house for him to get comfortable, and I was just getting rid of the smell months later.

I pointed to where the little bugger was headed so hubby took a shot, then another, and another, and another. He didn't move after the first shot but I guess you can't be too careful with a skunk. We went over to where the varmint lay to find the snow bank was yellow. He'd sprayed but it wasn't terrible-smelling at all; I guess maybe because it went into the snow instead of the air. I'd never seen one of these creatures up close so I was like the little kid that stands back with their nose curled up, not quite sure if they should step closer or not.

The Cowboy was pointing out to me where the scent glands were and how his feet were shaped so I could recognize the track, blah blah blah. I said, "Wow, look how long his claws are." So the cowboy took the barrel of his gun and poked the skunk to flip him over. Now you might not believe the events that I'm about to tell you but I swear on my life it's the exact truth! For those of you that were rooting for the skunk, no he didn't get up and scamper off; my husband never misses. The bugger did get revenge though.

I looked at the Cowboy after he poked the skunk with the gun and he did what most men do. He smelled it...what is it about testosterone that makes men smell the most horrid things and then take it over to their friend and make him smell it? Sorry, got off subject.

"Ahhh yuck!" he exclaims.

"Duh," I reply.

So then he takes his gloved hand and wipes off the barrel of the gun. He smells his glove!

"Ahhh yuck!" he again exclaims.

"What the...?" I ask in amazement.

Then he wipes his glove on his coveralls!

"Ahhh yuck!"

"Are you a freakin' idiot??!!!??!!!" I ask in the most loving and nurturing tone possible. Okay, not really.

He then looked at me like a little kid who's just been caught covered in mud in his church clothes and doesn't know what to do next. Pretty sure at this point, I was laughing so hard I peed a little!

I gave the Cowboy strict instructions to not touch me or he'd know what a "dry spell" was all about. We got back to the house and he started to go inside to take off his coveralls. I quickly stopped him at the door. He was stripping down on the porch for the next two weeks.

What's the moral of this story? Well, there really isn't one. Most people know that skunks smell. I just thought it was about time you laugh at the Cowboy instead of me since his "moments" are fewer and farther between than mine.

"YOU CAN'T SAVE THEM ALL," I WAS TOLD AS TEARS welled up in my eyes. The Cowboy couldn't even see me but he knew I was about to cry over the calf that lay dead on the barn floor. "We did our best to help her. That's all anyone can ask." It was true; we did do everything but it was still heartbreaking.

The Cowboy called me and told me to get everything ready; we were going to pull "that" heifer. I knew who "that" was: #226. We'd been watching her for several days now. I was relieved that the call was coming in the day and not at 3:00am. I rounded up all the gear and the munchkin and we were soon out the door and headed for the barn.

The Cowboy and I have pulled too many calves to count and too many heifers to remember. A lack of a heifer bull was the problem way back when. Mother

Nature was the problem with this one so many years later on this ranch. She looked like an alright heifer; not too tiny, not too small of hips, just an average heifer.

We had her in the head-catch in no time and went to work on pulling the calf. She wasn't pushing at first but with some encouragement, she started to help a little. It was soon clear that there wasn't any progress made. We then went "fishing" - in other words, we went in to feel the position of the calf. My smaller hands were no help this time as my arms weren't long enough. By this time, the boss man, who conveniently enough happened to be a vet, had arrived. He too went fishing and could barely touch the head.

The calf had its head turned back. This means that the usual front feet first with head in the middle didn't apply. The front feet were pointed out with a bit of a twist and the nose was pointing towards the ground and up and over his shoulder. It didn't help that every time someone had a hand on the calf's head to get it straightened out, the calf would pull back. It was a mess on every level you could imagine.

Once we finally got the calf straightened out, the momma laid down while we were pulling. So we started pulling from the ground. She was too small. Boss Man had to do the bovine equivalent of an episiotomy; he had to cut to make room for the calf. Finally, we got the calf out.

The momma just lay there, not really knowing what just happened. The calf just lay there, never knowing what just happened. The heifer calf never took a breath. Momma still laid there, relieved of her burden and pain, not wanting to get up. She was a good momma; she never bellowed, never tried to fight us, never freaked out like some heifers do. It just wasn't meant to be.

Losing a calf is never easy, but losing one that you've tried so hard to save is worse. When you step out of a barn covered in baby goo and blood and there's a live calf on the ground, it's a great day and worth a high-five. When you step out of a barn covered in baby goo and too much blood, to see the clouds have rolled in and it's raining and knowing there's a dead calf, it just makes you want to cry. And I did.

SEEMS TO ME THAT MOTHER NATURE HAS A FEW things backwards sometimes. Cows are fat and happy when it is sunny and popping out calves when it's nasty. This was the case when we found "Lucky". It was a name that was well-earned.

We still had a couple of feet of snow on the ground in spots and ice was still thick in some places on the river. The old cows were rolling right along and we didn't have many problems with them at all. I was constantly peering out through my binoculars checking any suspicious activity. We had all the "heavies" up by the house so I could see most of them from my front porch.

There's always one that sneaks past you though. She doesn't show any signs of calving any time soon.

Well, #232 was just like that; a little more secretive than the rest. She made her way down to a patch of trees near the river and thought that would be a good place to pop.

I saw her down there and watched her for a while until she had a red calf. The calf was up in no time and the two were just happy as could be. I told the Cowboy so we made a quick trip down there and they were just right as rain. The next day we were busy sorting more heavies, sorting off pairs and moving all these into their own pastures. As it would turn out, the pairs were going into the pasture where #232 and calf already were. One less pair we had to move.

The following day we noticed that #232 didn't come up to hay and she still hadn't introduced her little red calf to the rest of the nursery. She seemed happy enough, just grazing down by those trees, so we didn't bother to mess with her. Later that afternoon, she started bawling. This isn't uncommon. I've learned cows are not very smart sometimes and they forget where they put their calf down for a nap. Their bag gets full of milk and they go looking for the baby for relief. So then they start bawling to find them. Silly, I know. All you can say sometimes is...stupid cow.

By early evening I'm starting to get a little concerned. So I tell Cowboy all that has been happening and he says to go check. I then make a good argument that if something is wrong, I won't know what to do. So we hop in the truck and head down there together. It wasn't long till we saw #232 frantically searching for her calf. It was now official; she had lost him...stupid cow.

She was in and out of the trees, up and down the river bank, and all along the irrigation ditch. The irrigation ditch ran almost parallel to the river separated by a built-up bank to prevent flooding from the spring run-off. The ditch was mostly full of snow and often covered in a six-inch thick layer of ice. The Cowboy and I went up and down, over and across the ditch and the river looking for the calf. Meanwhile, the cow freaked out and got the heck outta dodge. So now we didn't have much hope of finding the little bugger since now he didn't have a momma calling for him.

Cowboy yelled for me to come back. It was dark anyway and even he didn't know how else to find the calf. As I was walking back, I heard the diesel fire up and I was feeling pretty discouraged. I just knew in the morning we'd probably find a half-eaten carcass from predators. Then I thought I heard something.

I stopped only 30 yards from the truck. Cowboy got out and yelled, "What?" I yelled back for him to shut off the truck. I told him I heard something. He thought I'd been in the whiskey barrel and was hearing things. I heard it again. Just the faintest of cries, so pitiful and soft I wouldn't have heard it if I didn't have estrogen. Yes, that mighty force of needing to mother something, anything, even if it was a calf.

I started to resemble that frantic #232 or a mother in Walmart searching for a child that wandered; they both looked about the same. My husband on the other hand still thought I was certifiably nuts. He just stood there waiting for me to wear out or give up. Obviously he still had a load to learn about estrogen! I yelled for all I was worth, "He's here! I found him!!! He's under the ice!"

Sure enough, he was lying in the ditch, feet barely visible pointed toward the opening, body soaked in two inches of water, and stuck. The opening was only about a foot tall and two or three feet wide. He wasn't stuck in a well but he was still the "baby Jessica" of calves. Now, this is the time when you hope there's enough useful crap in the bed of your pickup to deal with such a crisis. I haven't met a rancher yet that couldn't solve the world's problems with the contents of his pickup.

I stayed with the calf while the Cowboy was gathering supplies from the truck. A sledge hammer and a blanket; not the best of tools but not the worst either. Cowboy grabbed the hammer and made a quick thud on either side of the calf. He gave a little bawl from the weight of the ice so we had to work fast. Cowboy squatted down, grabbed the ice and lifted while letting out a huge groan. I shimmied between his legs and grabbed the calf's back feet and started to drag him out. This wasn't easy, especially when I was trying to hurry. Well, I ended up crawling in the ditch with him. I gave him a giant hug around his ribs and planted my feet and we worked our way out backwards with the calf on top of me. Once we were clear, Cowboy dropped the huge chunk of ice with a thud.

Then two more thuds. We both fell back; Cowboy from the strain and me looking this calf in the eye because I still was afraid to let go. All three of us were out of breath.

We wrapped up the calf and he sat on my lap for the truck ride up to find his momma. I didn't mind too much that we both smelled like wet calf, fish, dirt, and poop. We quickly found her but he went running off to suck anything that would stay still long enough. She finally found him and they were both happy as clams. Cowboy said, "That's one lucky little bugger".

If that's what it takes to name a calf Lucky, I hope there is never need for that name again.

2

NOW THAT THEY ARE HERE...

Once the calving starts, tagging also starts. Some people choose not to do this step but we always have. The idea is to catch the calf either shortly after birth or within a couple of days. We always gave the little buggers a "once-over" to make sure they were healthy, check their umbilical cords, occasionally give them a vitamin shot to put an extra spring in their step, put a tag in their ear that matches their momma and send them on their way. Most of the time, as long as they were healthy, the whole process took about three minutes. The less time away from momma, the easier it is for baby.

More often than not, everything goes off without a hitch. It is those times when it does not that are the most memorable. This particular time there was a big storm that had rolled through so we were unable to tag the calves. It wasn't the bad weather that kept us away; it was swollen ears. When it gets really cold, a calf's ears will swell up. If you tag it while swollen, it can cause permanent damage to the ear in addition to excessive bleeding and possible infection. After the swelling goes down the tag usually falls out anyway and you end up starting over, only the second time is harder. Due to the storm, we had about 35 calves to tag that day.

We knew we'd be busy for quite a while so we had to take our almost one-year-old daughter to the neighbor's house for the day and her first time away from us. On this fine day, the Cowboy told me to ride the Blue Mare. Since I was having flashbacks from the "Mellow Yellow" ride a few years earlier, I was very skeptical. I knew she was a good broke horse but I also knew that she could and often times would jump five feet sideways if spooked by a horse-eating plant.

We headed out and I knew my job. Cowboy would rope the calf if necessary and I was to push the cow away and keep my horse between her and my Cowboy while he tagged the calf. Not too hard; I'd done it several times before, just on a different horse. Yes, well, that might have been the key to all this. We spotted our first pair; the calf was taking a nap, I pushed momma off, and things were good. Then the calf realized there was a person restraining him and started to bawl. Needless to say, momma came running. She then started bellowing. This is not a typical mooo or even an "I lost my calf" bawl. It's more like a growl/guttural utterance/demon posses-sion of a cow-type sound accompanied by head shak-ing, dirt throwing, and charging like a freight train. My horse hadn't really seen a demon-possessed cow before so she backed away a little. In return, I gave her a little poke to urge her forward again.

It's at this point in the story where things get a little fuzzy, or maybe blurry is a better word. Since there was a blur of cow coming toward me, a blur of my horse jumping and taking off, and a blur of me trying to stay in the middle of the horse. Somewhere in the background was a blur of descriptive words coming from the Cowboy aimed at anything that would listen: the calf, the cow, the horse, the wife, or whatever.

If you're keeping track, we still have 34 calves to tag. So I traded my saddle for a four-wheeler since the mare wasn't ready to perform an exorcism and we didn't have the time to deal with it right then. I'm also not afraid to say when I've reached my limits of horsemanship either. So now my job was, once he had the calf, I come in and keep the cow off Cowboy. Now, by this I mean I have a sorting stick and moving my feet to protect me, and an occasional rock I can throw. So we get to rolling on these calves with no major problems. Most mommas are mad but won't "try" you or, in other words, try to eat you.

Then there was #162. Her calf didn't even make a sound and she was on us like flies on poop. She was bellowing and charging. I stood between her and my husband and cocked my arm, ready for a baseball swing. Most of the time if you just poke a cow with a stick or wave your arms around, they will watch what you're doing but leave you alone. Not her. I swear the ground shook as she came after us. Probably not, it was probably my heart trying to jump out of my throat. She was quite literally going to stomp my husband to death.

Swing...I caught her right in the nose. She backed off for about ten seconds. Yeah, that was all. Most cows will just stand there mad but won't try it again. Well, let me just say once again...stupid cow. She came after us again, more mad than the first time. Now I'm yelling descriptive words, trying to get the Cowboy to hurry up. But he was having a bit of a hard time since his horse was starting to get nervous at this second charge, too. Now Cowboy had to get the rope off the calf's feet, finish giving the vaccine, and keep a hold of his horse while a freight train is coming at us.

I'm still screaming at this cow, ready to swing, wanting to run, but not wanting my husband to get hurt in the process. *Swing*...She stumbles a bit and backs off shaking her head. Then, almost immediately, I'm getting yelled at - more like scolded but it felt like a yell - by Cowboy who's standing behind me now. What the heck is going on?

Well, with my fabulous aiming skills, or the severe lack of such, I thwacked her just below the eye and down her face to her nose. So now she's walking around squinting and I'm getting yelled at that she could lose her eye and to never do that again. Then I did what I usually do in those situations; I burst out crying. I was apologizing to the calf for needing to be tagged, to the cow for hurting her even though she wanted to kill me, to the ranch for even being here, and to everyone and everything that might listen. I then turned to my Cowboy. "I didn't mean to hit her there! She was coming after us and wouldn't stop. I'm sorry...but the stupid cow was trying to eat me for dinner!" Little did I know, but in a few days we would be dealing with an angry cow on a whole different level than this one; the infamous P242.

There is a saying that the Cowboy is a big fan of: Wild Cowboys make Wild Cows. I believe this to be true as well. It's a proven fact that the more you "Cowboy" a cow by chasing, running and just generally stressing it out, the wilder they become. It's the age-old "flight or fight" mechanism that's built in. However, I also believe that no matter how quiet you are around some cows, they were just born to be wild.

P242 was her number and "That wild one" was her name. We left her alone on purpose thinking that she might someday chill out and get used to being around people. That didn't work out so well. Calving season was upon us full swing and there she was, calf on the ground and afterbirth still hanging out. She was one of those cows that ate people for breakfast. We tried to tag the calf on horseback only to have her running into our horses and almost causing a wreck. So we opted for using the truck as a shield so, if necessary, the Cowboy could slip underneath while I was hoping she didn't crawl up on the flatbed with me. We got the little bugger tagged and left them both alone.

A couple days went by as we watched her from afar. She still hadn't shed the placenta, also known as afterbirth. This was a big problem because infection can set in, releasing toxins in the blood. If it's not removed, the cow can die. Normally, we would have brought her in the next day but, since she was "the wild one", we were hoping for a miracle.

When we would check cows at night we usually just hopped on the four-wheeler. I guess the sound of it just made her mad. All the other cows were just fine, never even getting up from their beds to look at what we were doing. She, on the other hand, must have had a personal vendetta with it as she would find us and chase us around the whole pasture, bellowing the whole way. So when we saw the afterbirth, we knew it would have to be done on horseback.

I guess you can imagine how thrilled I was about this. Trying to get a wilder than wild cow up to the barn to doctor her on horses that she's not afraid of wasn't exactly high on my to-do list. My thought was to let the stupid cow die. Compassionate, I know, but I didn't have much use for her after she'd chased me so many times and went after my horse. To me, there's no sense in keeping a mean cow around when there's plenty of good ones out there that could just as easily call this place home. She needed to "get on the bus", get down the road, and become someone else's human-eating problem. The Cowboy said that we couldn't just let her die, being the constant cattleman that he is. With much protesting from me, we were saddled and ready to go tackle this wild cow problem.

Quicker than we thought, we got her all the way up to the upper trap close to the barn through a series of smaller and smaller pastures designed to funnel up to the wooden corrals. It was one of those, "Wow, that wasn't nearly as hard as I thought it would be" moments. We had to bring a few other pairs with her but no big deal. We were almost to the wooden corrals when she noticed most of the other cows were trailing behind. Then, for no real reason since we were far behind not wanting to put too much pressure on her, she decided it would be a good idea to exit stage left. Through the five strands of barbed wire she went. Not over, not under, but through without even so much as a speck of blood. So now we have to get her back into the smaller pasture instead of the 10,000 acre one in which she now stood. To make it worse, we can't use the trap alley anymore since there was a giant P242-sized hole in the fence.

After traveling all over the country, we finally got her back in. Only a couple minutes later, she was headed in the direction of the barn. Exit stage right through another fence. This show is getting old pretty fast. Desperate times and wild cows call for desperate measures.

Again, I said, "Let her die."

The Cowboy, on the other hand, had dealt with these kinds before. He exhausted every trick in the book including using her calf as bait to get her up to the barn. I think she forgot she even had a calf because she didn't care one lick about him. So finally the Cowboy gathered up his rope and built a loop.

I'd never seen the Cowboy rope a cow before. Calves, oh sure, plenty. But he always said he hated to rope a cow especially by himself because, let's face it, I would be no real help in this adventure. Remember, wild cowboys make wild cows. Since we'd established that she was wild way before we came into the picture, he was a little more okay with it because he wasn't to blame for her wildness. I think it became "personal" now that she made extra work for him in the form of two giant holes in the fence. Either way, she still had to be doctored.

After a couple times of trying to get her roped the easy way, the Cowboy said, "Go get my other rope." So off to the barn I went, not all that fast either. I didn't really care at this point. It had already been a long day of stress and yelling over this stupid cow. I went up to the barn, tied up my horse, found the rope, and took my time. I led my horse through the gates, not being too concerned with the amount of time this took, and finally got back on. I walked my horse then trotted a bit until I reached the top of the hill. Then, just for show, I started to lope; that way he couldn't yell at me for taking too long since he could see I was going faster than a trot.

I finally get down to where I left him and it was a bit confusing. His horse was on the wrong side of the fence, just standing there. He was on foot screaming you don't want to know what. The cow was on the other wrong side of the fence with a rope around her neck. Hmmm, maybe I should have hurried a bit...nah. Let me fill in the blanks for you. I left. He roped the cow just as she went through the third fence. Now the cow was on one side of the fence and he was on the other. He kept a hold of her only because the Blue Mare wouldn't give up and squatted down against the pull of the rope like a champ. The cow then lay down from sheer exhaustion so the Cowboy released the pressure. He then got on the same side of the fence as her and waited for me. While waiting, he stepped off his horse to try to adjust the rope around her neck so she couldn't choke herself to death. Hmmm, not what I would have done.

It turns out, most of the time I was gone, he was being chased on foot by a not-so-exhausted P242. It came down to this....while he was getting back on his horse, the cow was getting up. The horse saw this, got nervous, and started to shy a bit. The Cowboy saw what was going on and figured it was better to let go of the horse than to have her hit them both and cause a huge wreck. So horse and rider scattered in opposite directions with cow in tow behind rider. Luckily, horse didn't go far, just out of the way of the cow which is what rider should have done in the first place.

At this point, I'm getting my butt chewed for taking so long and how he could have been killed or worse. My argument was, "Why in the hell did you get off your horse? You know darn well she'd take you. If you'd never got off, you wouldn't be in this situation. Maybe you'll think about that next time you try to commit ranching suicide!" While I thought this made perfect sense, the Cowboy thought otherwise.

Finally after another hour or so, we led her up to the barn. We were not able to convince her to go through the chute though. We had to tie her up and rope her back feet just to doctor her. I can't even describe to you the smell of half-expelled, decaying, covered in poop, three-day-old afterbirth. My gag reflex was working that day for sure. We got her uterus all cleaned out, medicine administered, and turned her loose in the alleyway of the barn. The Cowboy went to let her out and she wouldn't leave! We had her calf right there waiting for her but she wouldn't leave the barn! So we left and came back after an hour or so. P242 was just bound and determined to be a menace to society. Finally, after failed attempts of using himself as bait and getting her to try to chase him out, the Cowboy had had enough of her for one day. He brought in the four-wheeler and chased her out; well, more like he butted heads with her. She finally backed down from the steel bumper and went out. I think a huge sigh of relief came over the whole ranch.

P242 made a full recovery. She went on to raise her calf through the summer and got shipped off that fall due to her bad attitude and fence-shredding ways. I'm pretty sure someone somewhere is looking at her thinking "Wild Cowboys make Wild Cows". Well I got news for you, poor rancher man. Some cows are just wild.

SUMMER

Long days. Playful calves. Gardens in bloom. Tiny foal whinnies. Old friends gathered for new memories. Bellowing bulls. Children splashing in water. Hanging clothes drying in the breeze. A mist of fly spray on a slick-haired horse. Memories made and yet to be.

"Don't fall in love with me. I'll break your heart. I'm only here for the summer." I remember those words that my Cowboy spoke as if it were yesterday. I nodded in reply, made light of the conversation and moved past the subject. I knew full well he felt differently even if he didn't know it yet.

1

THE GOOD, THE BAD, AND THE HEADLESS

The lazy days of summer. I'm positive they don't exist on a ranch. Amazingly enough, the people on ranches make time to enjoy the season. Most of the time, summer fun still shows up in work clothes but is present nonetheless.

There is a name for the end of spring that heralds the beginning of summer. Branding season. This time is when friends and neighbors come out of the woodwork to help each other. Everyone is happy to shed their winter coveralls, O. B. gloves and medicine bags in exchange for new ropes, hot irons, good food, cold beer, and making fond memories.

The need for good neighbors, both to have them and be one, is felt greatly during a branding. In the ranching world, "neighbor" is a loose term. It might be the person who lives next to you but that might be five or thirty miles away. We've been lucky to have good ones and have been kept on our toes by the bad ones.

One summer after finishing up some last-minute food items, I zipped over to the branding pen. When I pulled up, things were just getting going and some mommas were being sorted off. The kiddos were hanging out on a flatbed trailer out of the way and perfectly content. The calves were bawling in the pen, the mommas were milling around and bawling outside the pen. Most of the horses were tied up outside the pen with a couple hobbled while everyone was getting things set.

The combination of a few of these things is what started the chain of events. A momma cow trying to find her calf a little too close for a colt's comfort, the colt in turn starting to crow-hop through the row of tied-up horses which in turn freaked out said cow who ran away, thus freaking out the other colt that was hobbled who in turn showed everyone how easy it is for a horse to not only run but buck with hobbles on and subsequently cover quite a bit of county without much effort. The first colt continued on his path of hops and squeals heading for the flatbed trailer.

Maybe I would have been a better horsewoman or tougher ranch wife if I had stepped in front of the horse and grabbed a rein and held him. Well, I didn't. I jumped on the flatbed, placed the munchkin and her two-year-old buddy behind me, and pulled up another little man onto the trailer. Then I threw a hand up to catch the attention of the closer-hopping colt to divert his direction. Not heroic by any means; I was just a mother hen paranoid about my little chicks.

Anyway, it was all over and done and no one was worse for the wear. A little while later, horses were back in place and calves were being roped, wrestled, vaccinated and branded. I wasn't able to stay too long as I had to get back to finish up the food and setting up for hungry cowboys and cowgirls.

Soon everyone was driving through the front gate, hungry from a day's work. We ate lunch, laughed, swapped stories, and sat around enjoying the sunshine and great weather. The beer held out long enough that some stayed for Round 2 and we grilled up some more burgers and ate again. It was a great time all around and it's too bad that branding season only comes around once a year. It's great to have such wonderful neighbors.

On the other hand, it's not so great to have not-so-great neighbors. We found this out during a very long, busy day on the ranch. It was one of those days that you leave in the dark and come home at dusk, only to turn around and leave again and not get home until well after dark. The Cowboy and two more guys he had helping him were busy sorting, shipping and receiving new pairs that we took care of for someone else. All week it had been raining and snowing so it was difficult for the semi-trucks that were hauling the cattle to get in and out. It was a mess. The guys were wet, cold, muddy and tired.

It was then that they were reminded that not all neighbors are as helpful or as friendly as those that we were with exactly one week prior. The neighbor was mad about all the trucks in and out and threw a fit over an easement that we used. The piece of dirt in question was only about one foot wide and the trucks weren't even using it by staying on the main road. When you are faced with situations like that, meaning the neighbor holding a gun while you stand next to the police officer, it just makes you more thankful for the good neighbors.

Like neighbors that bring you 20 pounds of potatoes just because someone gave them too many. Or neighbors that call you up to grill burgers but tell you not to forget your horse because we're going to rope first. Or when someone just shows up and brings you plants from their garden because they heard you were just starting out and thought you would need help with yours in the first year. Or when they volunteer to watch your little munchkin so you can have a "date" that involves gathering and trailing cows off the mountain.

We've been very blessed to have some great neighbors in the different places we've lived. I think that's one of the great things about ranching. Even if you haven't known your neighbors for very long, it's a great comfort to know that they are there if you need them and you'll be there for them, too. It's such a wonderful feeling for people like the Cowboy and me that don't always have family close by. Neighbors become family.

THE SUMMER AFTER MY FIRST LAMBING SEASON, I WAS on a quest to purchase some sheep of my very own.

My Cowboy was okay with caring for sheep as a part of a paycheck on a cattle ranch but wanted no part in owning them. I told the Boss Man about my intentions and I soon learned he was willing to help me get my start in the sheep business.

The Boss Man gave the Cowboy a deal for me. He said if I was able to nurse some of these lambs that had a mineral deficiency back to health, we'd work a deal so I could keep one or two. Wahoo! I was so excited to nurse me some sheep! The next morning I was brought two little girl lambs. One was much worse off than the other. The smaller of the two was weak and a little shaky on her feet. The other was completely down. She wouldn't even try to get up.

So three times a day I would tend my flock. I gave them each 4-cc of corn syrup. The weaker of the two, I gave a raw scrambled egg. I had to move her to give her water, put her in fresh grass so she could graze, and put her in shade in the heat of the day. On day two, the smaller but stronger of the two began to explore the yard. She would wander around the shop, graze and overall just annoy the dogs. She would follow the munchkin around and come when I called. I think the grain bucket could take most of the credit for her loyalty; I'm not claiming to be a sheep whisperer or anything.

Every evening I would put them in their makeshift hospital pen where they'd bed down safe and sound for the night. On day four, the weaker of the two was again laying down when I went out in the morning. I picked her up to move her to fresh grass and she actually flinched her legs. I then worked with her for a few minutes and eventually she stood on her own. I coaxed her to take a few steps with a handful of grain. Other than a few mishaps throughout the day, she was up and moving on her own. She was pretty shaky at times, but she was trying and getting better.

I was so proud of my little flock. I was even more proud of my nursing abilities. Then one morning we heard coyotes and our dogs were letting us know about it. The Cowboy and I ran out of the house toward the sheep pen. I was clad in a teddy bear night-shirt, flip-flops, and a gun. That sight alone was enough to scare off anything animal or human at five in the morning. The sheep were just where I'd left them the night before. They gave us a look that said, "What? Do you mind? Trying to sleep here."

The next morning is when I went from nursemaid and dutiful flock tender to Little Bo-Peep, without the happy ending. Yes, I'm the single most terrible sheepherder ever recorded in history. I lost my sheep. In the space of a half of an hour, they were swallowed by a black hole. That's my only theory. I searched high and low. I went everywhere on the four-wheeler. With a sheep-proof fence on three sides of us, where could they go? Seriously. Where? People don't just lose sheep.

Well, I do. If you have a sick lamb, just bring 'em on over. Rest assured I'll bring them back to full health. Be careful though because I'll lose them quicker than you can say "lamb chops for dinner". The

Cowboy couldn't help but poke fun at my tears. "They're just sheep."

I cried all the same. I cried when we fed sheep, I cried when I went to bed, and I cried when my munchkin said, "Help sheep, Momma?" She loved helping me take care of them.

A fact is a fact. I think my quest for owning sheep might be over. "Ranch wife" is my main title. However, "terrible sheepherder" has reluctantly been added to my resume.

Another title I've had to work at slightly less than "ranch wife" is "woman". As a woman, every once in a while I turn into a sappy girl and I need a little romance in my life. It's the nature of the estrogen beast. So one day when the Cowboy told me he could use my help, I jumped at the chance for a "date". A wise woman, Julie Carter, once wrote, "Always know there is absolutely no romantic intention when he pleadingly asks you to take a ride with him." I should have known better but I fell for it again.

My in-laws were in town so we had a babysitter for the munchkin. I got all "dressed up"...you know, jeans, long-sleeved shirt because deer flies are the devil, and hat. This wasn't the type of date where the man opens the car door so instead he put my spurs on my boots and caught my horse. I was busy packing a diaper bag and moving the car seat when I noticed he even sprayed my horse with fly spray. Yes, these things count as chivalry in the world of a ranch wife!

I was done getting the munchkin ready so I saddled my horse. He has to really, really want something for him to be that romantic and saddle my horse for me. In no time at all, we were loaded and headed out the driveway. I told him thanks for taking me and he gave me a look that sealed the deal. He knew that I'd forgotten the guidelines. What a turd, luring me in with romantic notions!

Upon arrival, he gave me the general directions and layout of the pasture. The 100 or so pairs of momma cows and calves had broke through the fence and wandered into the sagebrush. There wasn't a gate to speak of so we had to bring them back through the hole in the fence. We rode together for a little while and then split off. It's funny how you don't have to be right next to someone but you can still feel close to them. I was having all kinds of flashbacks to the days when I was his only help and it was do or die. I was proud of myself for not asking 1,000 questions and just knowing what needed to be done.

I headed off at a trot, knowing full well I had a good distance to go until I hit the other fence line and also knowing that I had the slow horse. We were picking our way through the sagebrush when I remembered how much I love that smell. A warm breeze on your face, the hint of fly spray being sweated off your horse, the sweet smell of sagebrush as your horse brushes up against it, and the mountains in the distance...hmmm, little pieces of heaven. I was snapped out of my little daydream every time my horse thought it was easier to jump the sagebrush than go around it.

I looked up and thought a calf had climbed

through the fence but when I got closer, I saw it wasn't one of ours. Then I went to get a bull moving but he was a little lame so I left him and started on with the other cows. By this time, the Cowboy had pushed a couple off the hill and joined up with the rest of us. We continued pushing and sweeping without a word between us.

I only had one minor panic attack when I had to go through the herd of mares and babies to pick up a few cows that were hiding. I didn't have any problem with the mares; it was the stud that started to come after me and got a little too close for my comfort. When I yelled and he realized we weren't interested in his mares, he backed off. Yet another first for me; not going to lie, I was a little scared for a minute.

We finally made it to the hole in the fence and started the task of getting them through. I held the herd on the one side to keep them from running down the fence and missing the hole. The Cowboy kept pushing and sweeping. It was a slow process since only a couple could go through at a time but it went off without a hitch. I really wanted to trade jobs since I knew if they blew past the hole, I'd be the only thing to stop them from scattering to the four winds. Luckily, I only had one try me so I had to go after her and turn her back on the fence.

When we were done pushing cows and the fence was fixed, the Cowboy gave his horse a "good job" pat on the neck and a few words of encouragement. When we got back to the trailer, his dog got a "good boy". When we were back at the house over an hour after the fact, his wife got a "Yeah, you did alright. I didn't have to tell you what to do."

It's official, just in case I had any doubts before. There are no romantic notions intended when a cowboy says he needs your help. Don't get me wrong; we had a good time and laughed and joked and it was nice to just get out and ride alongside my husband. However, I've come to the conclusion that there are no romantic dates in the sagebrush.

"POOR KICKENS," MY THREE-YEAR-OLD MUNCHKIN SAID looking down at the freshly-butchered chicken. The Cowboy and I were divided on how to introduce our daughter to the "life and death" part of ranching. One of my first memories at about the same age as her was of a headless chicken chasing me down the driveway. I had a mind of, "Go play somewhere else."

He was of the mind of, "She needs to learn where our food comes from." He was right and I knew it so she stayed.

It wasn't nearly as bad as I thought it would be. Having said that, I must admit I wasn't doing all the dirty work either. We only butchered two as a "trial run" kind of thing. The Cowboy must have felt bad for my ignorance and actually helped me a bunch. Much more than he first said he would. After a "wring" of the neck, there wasn't even any flopping or running or anything. In my daughter's words, "swing 'em like a rope (swish swish)". She then went back to riding her bike.

The now-headless chickens were hung up to bleed out while the water finished heating up. After the Cowboy dunked the first one, we hung it back up and I was off and plucking. Repeatedly I was told to take off my bright yellow rubber kitchen gloves and construction dust mask but I wouldn't have any of it. Admittedly, it did take me longer to pluck a chicken than it did the Cowboy but I'd rather chalk that up to inexperience, not the gloves.

During the plucking, the munchkin got curious again and came to investigate. She inspected the chicken and stated, "Chicken have owie. Him have no head." She then went back to more important things like playing with baby kittens and feeding the rest of the chickens.

We had a box full of feathers and heads, now we had to gut them. When I say "we", I mean that I helped hold the chicken to make it easier for the Cowboy to gut. Again, the child was curious and watched with a wrinkled nose. I'm quite proud of myself for not gagging until the second one was in the de-gutting process. Guess what got me? It was the mixture of the hot gut smell with the suction noise kicker. I didn't let go, though; I gagged and held the chicken at the same time. That's dedication!

I carried the chickens into the house to wash, weigh and wrap. We kept one for ourselves and the bigger one went into the freezer to sell. They weighed in at 3.75lbs and 4.25lbs. A little lighter than I thought they'd be but still a good weight.

A couple days later, I made chicken and noodles

with our home-raised chicken. The munchkin watched as I prepared and put it in the pot to boil. She was asking about the dead chicken so I tried to explain that sometimes we kill chickens so we have food to eat, just like the chickens kill grasshoppers so they can eat. She left and went to play. I heard her playing with a box and overheard her talking to herself. "Here's a box for the kicken heads, kicken feet, kicken fedders, and kicken guts. Now frow it away and eat da kicken."

The Cowboy was right all along. Kids take things much better than we give them credit for. Sometimes I forget how black and white their world is. She knows to be nice to all animals, not just chickens, and how to care for them while they are with us. She also knows that chickens eat grasshoppers to live and we eat chickens to live. I'd say that's a pretty good grasp on life in general for a three-year-old.

2

HORSING AROUND

The bill of sale read "one grey gelding." As a favor to my uncle that was putting on a horse sale, my dad consigned a few horses. I was asked to ride a four-year-old paint gelding named Reddy Bear. It was a small sale but had a good showing nonetheless. As is the norm, most of the horses being offered in the sale were being ridden in the bigger arena. Of course there were many potential buyers looking on, summing up each horse.

"Reddy" was doing alright until he thought it would be a great idea to "hog-fart" around. This is a term used by many horse people to describe a horse that is trying to buck but not really getting the job done because his back feet don't really leave the ground. Still, it's not cool when they do this, at least not in my book when I'm the one that's on board. So after his little hops and skips we continued riding like nothing happened. Of course my mom, being the eternal biggest fan of her child, was cheering, "You go girl, ride 'em!" in the background. I wasn't sure if I should be embarrassed or not. I really didn't want to draw any attention to any of it for fear of scaring off a buyer. But who has the heart to tell their mom that?

So through all this hubbub going on, I noticed an older cowboy riding a striking grey horse. I instantly thought how my Cowboy would look on this noble steed and how he's always said he likes a nice grey horse. I think it stems from the love affair my husband has with "Lonesome Dove" as he can quote almost the entire movie randomly. At any rate, I just knew this horse would fit the bill. So I mustered up the guts to get on this horse, which I don't usually do as I get so nervous on horses I don't "personally" know, and try him out. I figured if I could ride him, the Cowboy was sure to get along with him. He works his magic with problem horses and colts every day; this mount would be a vacation for him.

As luck would have it, that grey horse didn't sell. The owners wanted more money than anyone was willing to bid so he was a "no-sale". This is where years of bartering at garage sales worked in my favor. I went to the truck where the grey horse was "parked" and started talking shop. Before I knew it, I had him agreeing to half the price that he was "no-sold" for. This might have been a clue to the seasoned horse person but the shopper in me was excited at a deal. Turns out, they really wanted to get rid of this grey horse.

He loaded in the trailer like a dream and was a well-mannered gentleman. He was built right, had good pedigree papers, and rode great for me at the sale. As his luck would have it, the Cowboy couldn't get right on his new steed due to being busy with other horses and day-to-day life.

So Ike was his new name and a pasture full of belly-deep grass was his home. When the Cowboy was finally able to devote some time to Ike, his first words to me were, "I thought you said this horse was broke." His second phrase to me went something like "Don't ever buy ME a horse without me being around. Don't ever buy ANY horse without me being around. Better yet, don't EVER buy a horse. Leave that to me."

So finally after some prodding from me, the Cowboy finally admitted that this horse was okay but he needed a bunch of work to get him riding good. So began the journey of what I like to call Ike's evolution. The Cowboy was soon getting along just fine with him and was using him almost every day. They went out gathering cows, team roping and just riding.

The Cowboy went out of town for a few weeks off and on, helping out a friend build some fence. I was huge prego - eight months - and the doctor wouldn't let me ride anymore so the horses got fat and sassy off good green grass. We also had an 80-acre field of alfalfa next to our house. We had a single-strand fence around the yard and I would turn out the horses during the day to graze and "mow" my lawn. I was waddling around outside, planning out my garden, when I noticed I was short one grey horse. He had figured out that if he put his head under the wire he could lift it up or he'd find a low spot and just step over and he was free to graze on the "good stuff"...the alfalfa.

Now, if you don't currently or have never owned a horse, let me explain a bit about the difference between grass and alfalfa. Both are a great source of nutrients that horses need. In the winter, we usually feed a mix of grass and alfalfa hay. As we know, even in humans, too much of a good thing can be bad. In the case of this grey horse, he seriously needs to go to AEA: Alfalfa Eaters Anonymous. He gets a whiff of it and falls off the wagon. One little bite of it and he's wiggin' out for days. It really is his crack. He's a total junkie. So until they make Ritalin for horses, he's off the stuff for good.

This is how his "escape artist" days started. My patchwork fence repairing jobs were not cutting it. So when the Cowboy got home, we went to building a better fence. Then the aerial shows began. He was at least smart enough not to try the wire. The wooden gate was his favorite. He was so sneaky about it, too. He'd stand flat-footed a few feet away from a gate that was a bit over five feet tall and clear it without a sound. Let me just say this horse is 14.3 hands tall which is 59 inches from ground to withers. The first time I saw that I just had to laugh. Is it even possible to keep this horse in a fence? Ike soon turned into Grey Horse; his name was taken away as he was demoted for bad behavior.

Shortly after all these escapes kept occurring, our daughter was born. So riding Grey Horse was again put on the back burner. A couple weeks later, the Cowboy announced he was going to ride Grey Horse to the neighbor's house for coffee. This was a few miles away and he figured by the time he got there, Grey Horse would have worked out all the bugs and alfalfa. I watched from the driveway as the Cowboy stepped on. Somewhere in the back of my mind I thought, "This can't end well." Well at 6:30 am, just off a back road in Wyoming, Grey Horse got his crack - also known as alfalfa - taken away and he was swollen up mad at the world.

The horse was soon saddled up and ready to go even if he was mad at the world and every living thing on it. The Cowboy stepped on and made a few "warm-up" circles. It was very evident by the way Grey Horse was traveling that he was about to blow. Just by the slight hump in his back, the look in his eye, the swish of his tail, and the ever-telling snorts he was letting out, you could tell it was building.

As the Cowboy looked at me and said, "See? Not so bad," it happened. This wasn't a "hog-fart" around episode. This was full-out war in Grey Horse's mind and he was packing heat in both barrels. All those former fence dodging aerial antics proved small in comparison to the show he gave me. He looked as rhythmic as a well-trained bucking horse. You could set your clock to his jumps. Front hooves hit the dirt....tick...body rolls up to the air...tick...lifts his hips...tick...hind feet extend toward the sky...tick...hind feet hit the dirt...tick...jumps forward with front feet...tick...over and over and over again.

This horse doesn't know how to quit anything when he should. Neither does the Cowboy.

The scene took me back to when I first met him riding bucking horses. How my heart always skipped a beat until he was back safe on his own two feet. I remembered the knot in my throat when he didn't land on his feet. Then it hit me; it was just me here. The thought of my Cowboy not being able to ride Grey Horse hadn't crossed my mind. He'd never been thrown from a saddle horse before even if it was a colt that had never been ridden. What if he got caught up in a stirrup or something else? This wasn't a rodeo in an arena. There were no pick-up men on horseback to help get this rider off safe, no medics, and no other cowboys to help him to his feet. It was just me! What the heck would I do?

Lucky for me, I didn't have much time to ponder all these things. The Cowboy got Grey Horse shut down by pulling his head around to the side, disabling the bucking mechanism, so to speak. The stop of the show wasn't because of the horse. He was still going strong and had not even thought about weakening. The Cowboy always says that if a horse is squealing and making noise while they buck it's because they're giving it their all. If one is a quiet bucker, chances are they're just getting started. Guess which one Grey Horse was? Silent as a church mouse. After a few minutes to catch their breath, off they went to the neighbor's house as if the last five minutes had never happened. I still watched them for a couple of miles to make sure all was well.

They both returned safe and sound later that afternoon. I guess somewhere around mile three of four, they came to an agreement: Don't kill me and I won't kill you. They went on to gather some cows, rope a few steers and eventually have a nice ride home. This was a major improvement for Grey Horse. The last time the Cowboy tried to rope off of him, he flipped over backwards. You can normally rope off of him any day of the week but that day he just got mad and threw a fit.

Not too long after all this, we took a job up on "the mountain," as we call it. It was time for the fall gather and guess who was nominated for the ride? None other than Grey Horse. The ranch was about 80,000 acres, give or take a few, and the Cowboy was assigned one end of it.

"Either he's going to do something stupid and get me killed, or he's going to act stupid and I'm going to kill him." Those were the exact words of the Cowboy. Well, Grey Horse's luck held out and neither happened. He rode like a dream, ears always forward, eyes alert, and ready to travel some country. Together they rode 20 or more miles a day every day for two weeks straight. Grey Horse loved every minute of it. That horse just doesn't have any quit in him. Except when it comes to sheep.

We were just coming back from a wedding and had timed our days off perfectly to give us a few more to spare. As luck would have it, the Powder River Sheep Herders Fair was taking place. The Cowboy had been there several times before but not in recent years. He first started attending when he was in high school. He would help his best friend on his family's ranch all through the year and especially during the summers. They ran about 1200 cow/calf pairs and 8000 ewes. As much as he might not like to admit it, he knows just as much about sheep as he does cattle.

On our way to the big event, he was telling me how funny it was because every year there was at least one guy that would get bucked off. Apparently some horses just don't know what to think about sheep. So we finally arrive to enjoy the festivities only to be told that we are entered in the ribbon roping and Grey Horse had been hauled for the Cowboy to ride. Well, I can't deny that I freaked out a bit. I'd never even seen this thing done before and here we were fourth in line. Hmmm, well I guess my old saying still rings true...if I can pull a calf by sticking my hand up you know where, I guess I can do this too!

Before I knew it, we were in the arena being auctioned off for the calcutta. SOLD $25. Not the greatest price since most were in the hundreds and some were over $500. I guess no one wanted to gamble on us winning or even placing, for that matter. We went back out of the arena and I had to run to the truck. You see I was supposed to be watching in the stands. It was well over 100 degrees so I donned my capri pants and flip flops for the spectator sport. Well, no time to change, and nothing to change into anyway, so I improvised. I did have my boots in the back of the truck and a day-old worn shirt of the Cowboy's. I tucked my capris in my boots and buttoned up the husband's shirt since I didn't want the girls making a guest appearance out of the front of my tank top.

I now had a bunch of people telling me the rules and tricks of the trade. Start behind white chalk line at one end of arena, sheep is let out of chute from the opposite end, man riding horse ropes the sheep any way he can, woman runs up to sheep, grabs the ribbon off of said sheep and runs for all she's worth back to cross white chalk line. I watched the first three go off without a hitch. The times weren't the best, I was told, but it seemed all right to me. Then we were up and a sudden mantra went through my head....crap, crap, crap, what the heck are you doing? You've never even touched a sheep that wasn't in a pen at the county fair!

Well, as my foot crossed the line there was no time for panic; the sheep was already let out. This started one of the longest three minutes of my life. Cowboy took it easy so as not to excite both sheep and Grey Horse. I guess the sheep didn't get the memo that it was supposed to go nice and easy. Sheep freaked out like sheep do. Amazingly, Grey Horse was fine with all this. Then the Cowboy caught the sheep for a second. Sheep slipped through loop. Not before letting out a bawl like only a sheep can do. This is where Grey Horse didn't do so well.

If that horse could talk, I think we would have washed his mouth out with soap. The look, snort, squeal, and finally aerial show, pretty much sums it all up. So now, not only do I not know what I'm doing,

I'm stuck in the arena with a wild sheep, a bucking horse and a husband trying to yell orders for me to fix it all. Well, the extent of my fixing was me barely getting out of the way of one Grey Horse preoccupied with escaping a silly sheep.

Through it all, the Cowboy caught the sheep. Well, kind of. He threw his loop at its head and it ran through but came tight on his hind feet. So here I come running at this sheep before it gets loose. This causes a chain of events. Sheep bawls, horse freaks out, husband yells "hurry up," I grab ribbon and run in the opposite direction of the train wreck that's happening behind me.

All in all, we had made a clean run with a good time that was under four minutes. The next day we were auctioned off for $150. We ended up 3rd overall. There were many other festivities that went on as well. Sheep dog trials, sheep hooking (catch one out of a bunch with an old-fashioned sheep hook and bring across the line and tie three legs), and sheep-roping (like calf-roping in that you rope the sheep then get off your horse and go tie three legs, only you can't have your rope tied to your saddle, just thrown across) and a mutton cook-off were among the events.

It was great fun and there was even a big BBQ before the band started. As we sat down to eat after a hot day of dirt and fun, I had a question. The BBQ sandwiches were yummy so I asked, "What is this? Pulled pork?" Yes, yes, I did, I said it. The Cowboy looked as if he wanted to disown me. I was at a Sheep Herders Fair asking if the main meal was pork. Not my finest moment but I blame it on the heat and the scary sheep.

A couple of years and one child later, I decided to branch out and test myself. I signed up for a fund-raising trail ride for St. Jude's Hospital that was being put on by a friend of mine. I knew full well that the date was a bad one. My Cowboy had been talking about going roping the same day for months before I made these plans. This meant I wouldn't have my trusty horse Tango since he would be the one being used at the roping.

I knew I had to challenge myself and step out of my comfort zone. This could only mean one thing...pick a different mount. Blue Mare was the Cowboy's first choice for me but I've watched her spook at a chipmunk and jump five feet straight in the air. Since I don't have cat-like reflexes, I didn't want my horse to either. So I set my mind on Grey Horse.

After I drove two hours with my noble steed in the trailer, I was feeling good. I jumped him out, saddled up, and joined the group. In no time we were off for a good ride. I headed towards the front of the group since Grey Horse has a "let's cover some country" type of attitude that matches his pretty-quick walk. Without fail, every time another horse would get in front of him, he'd put his ears slightly back just so I knew he was annoyed. Then I'd let him out front for a bit and it was like flipping a switch; his ears forward, he would walk faster and he'd stop playing with the bit.

We went through some sagebrush, down some

hills, through the trees along the river, to Grand-mother's house...just kidding. Anyway, it was a good ride, lots of different scenery, no mishaps, just a good ride. We stopped at one point for a moment of silence for the children we were riding for and a time to share the names of people in our own lives that were affected by cancer. There were several names called out of loved ones. I spoke up for my husband, "Jayme Robert Pfaff, age 24". The Cowboy and Jay were best buds since they were in diapers but that is a different story. The good truly do die young.

After a prayer and a few tears, we moved forward. Before long we were back at the beginning and were ready to break for lunch. Cinches were loosened and horses were watered before we all headed down to eat. A silent observation of mine was no matter what level of rider at what event, be it equine or otherwise, you always see the livestock tended to before the people themselves.

We sat down for lunch and numbers were crunched and we passed out awards. Some of the riders had to leave and a few of us decided to stay and try a water crossing. I had a babysitter and a day off so of course I kept riding. The eight of us headed out and Grey Horse was happy to lead the way. I think he was looking for cows, but whatever. We made our way to the water and of course he had to drink first and then walk across. The other six riders followed suit with only mild hesitation from one. If you are counting, that leaves one rider on the other side. A paint mare named "Boo" not because of spooking but from the little girl in the Disney movie Monsters, Inc. Boo had made buddies with Grey Horse for most of the ride but she was an individual. When most horses would want to cross to get to the rest of the "herd", she was flexing her "Miss Independence" muscles. She could not care less that the rest of us were already across. Then a few other attempts were made at leading her across. None were working.

So my retarded butt thought well, she made buddies with Grey Horse, so maybe I can pony her across. If you don't know what "pony" means, it's when a rider takes the lead rope of another horse, with or without a passenger, and leads them around. So I spoke up and said that I would try. After all, I was riding a roping saddle and a horse that wasn't afraid to pull against pressure from all the roping and ranch work he has done. So we started out. On the first attempt, Grey Horse wasn't real sure what to do so he backed off of the pressure of the lead rope around the saddle horn. We made a circle and headed for the water again.

I'm not sure but it felt like that mare sat square on her butt. Well, Grey Horse got the idea and put his head down and pulled her forward into the water. Then she decided to jump the water which made her bump into Grey Horse. He wasn't really sure how to deal with that so he kind of jumped forward and took off. To his credit, he didn't blow up, not even a little bit. So here I am, half out of the saddle, holding a lead rope attached to a paint mare and trying to stop Grey Horse before running into other horses. Well, I got his one rein pulled around and he came to a stop, just without me on top. I saw it coming. While I was flying through the air, I was looking him in the eye with my back towards the ground and feet pointed to the sky. The worst part was, as I was flying he was still moving so the thought "tuck and roll" went through my head. Luckily, he stopped dead in his tracks so I didn't get stepped on. I hopped back up and gave him so much loving it wasn't funny. It wasn't his fault and I wanted him to know that. The other riders must have thought I was nuts but they didn't know what he could have done and didn't! He was a gentleman and stepped on the mare's halter so she didn't run off.

So after a few minutes of composure and check to make sure he wasn't hurt, I was back in the saddle. Now, let me just share this detail with you: we were on an island. There is nowhere to go but back through the water. To answer the question in your mind, no, the mare wasn't any more willing to cross it the second time than she was the first.

I gathered up Boo's lead rope once again and paused to take a deep breath. I nudged Grey Horse closer to the water and brought Boo with me. She was looking and trying to figure things out this time all by herself. I took Grey Horse into the middle of the water and Boo was still trying and even getting her feet a little wet. So I gave her some slack so she could figure things out and hopefully wouldn't jump this time. She did a little tap dance and even moved away from us a bit to find her own path. I gave a little tug when she looked like she was going to chicken out. I steered Grey Horse well out of the way up the slight hill. But I guess my idea of "well out of the way" and Boo's idea of it were two different things.

I turned back around to make sure Grey Horse was pointed in the right direction and heard some water splash. I didn't feel a bunch of slack in the rope, though, so I thought Boo was still headed straight. Right then I felt Grey Horse stumble a bit and saw him go down on his left knee. He stood back up and I didn't think anything about it. My next thought was, "Hmmm, why am I looking up at Grey Horse and Boo?" Yes, I was in the dirt, again.

Grey Horse sidestepped away from Boo since her lead rope was still over the saddle. I jumped up and went after my horse who stopped after a few seconds and a "whoa" from me. I gathered him up and started to look him over again. After a few "Are you okay?"s and "I'm fine"s, I was filled in on what happened. When Boo decided to cross, she jumped again. This time she landed on top of Grey Horse. Everyone thought that she had knocked me off. Instead, when she came down on him, he kicked out at her and kind of swung his body around. This is where I exited stage left and I didn't see it coming that time! He was just trying to defend himself against the creature that in his mind was probably trying to eat him!

Once I was filled in on the details, I gave Grey Horse another hug and looked him over again. Sure enough, he had two wet hoof prints on his butt, one on either side of his backbone. I walked him around a bit and he never took a bad step so I swung aboard again. We continued on for a while until some others needed to head back. I kept going and finished the loop.

I loaded Grey Horse up and we were off to pick up the munchkin. I called my sister and she said I should stay the night with my in-laws since I probably knocked my head harder than I thought since I wasn't making much sense. I then had to explain what the Grey Horse used to be like and what he could have done in that situation. Then I had to explain how much of a mental hurdle that was for me.

An accident many years before where a horse flipped over backwards on me along with becoming a mommy and I don't know what else made me a bit of a chicken when it came to riding horses. If I was riding my old man Tango, I was fine, but anything else I would freak myself out so much that I'd almost give myself a panic attack. So even taking a different horse that I'd only rode two times before a long ride was HUGE for me! Now trusting this horse to pony another across a creek, even bigger! Landing in the dirt, twice, you can't even imagine how proud of myself I was! It is official: Grey Horse has secured his name as Ike for such good behavior!

When I called the Cowboy to tell him everything that happened, his words of wisdom went something like, "Why did you do that? It wasn't his fault you fell off. If you'd have done it this way, you never would have wrecked." So, yes, I could have done things differently but the point was I did it. And got back on, twice!

Money I raised for St. Jude -- $360.00; Tylenol for sore muscles and bruises -- $2.50; Gaining confidence by landing in the dirt -- PRICELESS!

Now that time has passed and Grey Horse has been ridden many, many miles, you can just step on and ride off. His antics are fewer and farther between. He does still love to be hosed down on the hot summer days. He still curls his upper lip up if you rub his nose. He'll eat anything you give him. He knows when he's in trouble just by the tone of your voice. He finds a mud hole and rolls in it until you can't tell his true color for at least a week. He always knows when you're thinking of selling him because then he's sure to mind his P's and Q's until the thought goes away. He's still the first one to feel a storm coming on and runs around trying to get the other horses to play.

Just the other day, the herd came flying over the hill bucking and kicking the whole way. Guess who was in front? Grey Horse. When they all came to a halt, he was still running amuck, trying to get others to play with him. When rearing and kicking didn't do the trick, he took off like he was shot out of a cannon. It finally worked and the herd was off again. They were following Ike with his half-grown mane - short from the constant fence ducking - flying in the wind. Yes, I said Ike. The Cowboy told me the other day that a horse with that much unique character deserves a name. Even if he does get demoted again due to bad behavior to Grey Horse, somewhere deep down he'll always be Ike.

Teamsters. It's hard not to marvel at them. Gentle giant horses, happy to go to work. People patient enough to do things just for the joy of doing them. Old-fashioned. Nostalgic. Days gone by.

I saw some actual working teamsters cutting a hay field on my way home from town one day. I parked the truck, went down with my camera in hand to snap a few shots. I got to talking with them and they invited me to come to a different hay meadow they'd be cutting in a couple weeks. It promised to be more scenic. I jumped at the chance.

When we were finally able to connect, it was a joy. I was met at the gate by Robin, a tiny pixie little thing, tough as nails, leading this giant team in one hand. It's a wonder she isn't given bus tickets to keep in her pocket for when the Wyoming wind blows her to Nebraska and she needs a ride home. I've been around draft horses before, mostly just in the dude string, so it's been a while. You forget how little 5'3" is until you try to bridle one. I remember those moments of pleading with a giant horse to just cooperate with me. It really is pleading because there really isn't much you can do to force a draft horse into dropping their head. I always found that talking helps. Makes you look like a crazy person, yes, but usually gets the job done.

As I watched Robin bridle the horses, I snapped a few pictures. I couldn't help but wonder how many times a person has to hook up a team before not getting lost in all the leather lines, or tangled for that matter, and it going smoothly and not taking half the day before you actually get hooked to what you intend to pull. This is where the movie started to play in my head of all the ways I would tangle myself and end up pulling the wrong thing and find myself cinched up under the horse's belly getting ready to hold on to an almost one-ton runaway with hooves of fury. Seriously, these are the things I think about.

When I made it to the field, everyone was in full swing of cutting hay. All three teams were going strong. These gentle giants were hard not to love especially with names like Doug, Ted and Molly, just to name a few. The quiet was enveloping. It was everything that I love about Wyoming. The slight breeze whispering through the grass, bringing a whiff of sagebrush every now and then. The warm sun shining down while puffy summer clouds roll in over the hill.

There was hardly a sound to be heard. The giant horses were light as feathers across the field, barely even bending the grass as they walked through. While snapping pictures, I waited for the noise. There really wasn't any. A few creaks here and there from the old metal mowers, the occasional sneeze from a horse, and only when they got close could you hear the chatter from the mower's teeth. The grass fell to the ground as silent as it once grew.

Maybe it's not as soothing or as romantic when you're actually driving a team. I'd like to think that it is. Otherwise, why would anyone go to the trouble when there are plenty of tractors hanging around? I think the answer is the same as why we still use horses instead of four-wheelers for most of the ranch work. The Cowboy and I have both said many times that having a team would be nice, especially during the winter. When it's cold, a team always starts. Those cows get a little cranky when having to wait for breakfast because it's too cold for the tractor to start. I would love the sounds of it. The creaking of an old hay wagon, the swishing of the hay, the crunching of the snow packing under the horses' feet, and the munching from the crowding cows. It's the little things.

3

HURDLES AND A FULL CIRCLE

Have you ever heard someone say, "Sometimes in life, you just have to jump a few hurdles to get where you're going"? Who came up with that? How stupid. Maybe it's only stupid to me since I'd never be able to jump a hurdle...ever. My 5'3" short-legged, post-three-baby butt that now weighs in at one hundred blah blah blah would never make it up and over. I'd be the one chunky kid you see at a track meet that's just painful to watch as he comes to the hurdle and just knocks it over with his belly in an attempt to jump. Anyway, you get the idea, right?

Well, I've felt like there's been a whole string of hurdles set in front of me when it comes to the ranching life. I'm not complaining, just stating a fact. The Cowboy says I ask too many questions some-times. I don't know where he'd get that idea. Maybe it's just because I'd like to know how high the hurdle is before trying to jump.

- Hurdle #1: You want me to live how far from town? Now, I've never been much for big cities but I was a little fond of civilization. I didn't even have to be pizza-delivery close, just close enough to get in the car and be in town in like 15 minutes.

- Hurdle #2: You want me to walk 3/4 mile to and from the house because there's too much snow to plow? In the dark? When moose walk through our yard every night? When I can hear wolves howling on the next ridge? I don't really think I need to explain my reasoning for questioning the Cowboy's sanity on this one.

- Hurdle #3: You want me to be your only help? Us? Just us on this ranch? I've never done any of that before! Are you crazy? Me? Do that? I hope you know what you're getting yourself into.

- Hurdle #4: You want me to go where to find cows? The south pasture? Which way is that? Really, I don't know which way is south. Would I ask you if I did?

- Hurdle #5: You want me to stand in the gate so the 1300+ pound cow doesn't go out? Have you seen the size of that cow? How am I going to keep her from going out? Jump and make noise? How many times have I told you to put down the crack pipe, honey?

- Hurdle #6: You want me to stick my hand

where? Do what to that unborn calf? Shouldn't I have a pair of gloves on? What do you mean there's no time to run and get some gloves? Isn't there always time to put on gloves to keep your hands from getting icky?

- Hurdle #7: You want me to go move the bulls? What if they fight me? What if they don't want to move? Why aren't you coming with me?

- Hurdle #8: You want me to sort pairs with you? Can't I just run the gate? No gate? Why don't we just gather them all up and sort from the corrals? No corrals? Ahh crap...

- Hurdle #9: You want me to sit on this colt while you get it to moving? Where's the risk for you? Why am I the guinea pig?

- Hurdle #10: You want me to do all this other stuff while waddling around hugely pregnant? Really? Whatever happened to a woman's delicate sensibilities? Or going away for my confinement? Seriously, can't I just lie like a beached whale on the couch? No, I'm pretty sure the doctor didn't say staying active was good for me....

As you can imagine, those are just a few of the hurdles I've come face to face with. I'd like to tell you each one that was set before me, I negotiated with grace and ease but that's usually not how it went.

Sometimes I threw myself on the ground in protest; kicked, screamed and pounded the ground so much that the hurdle just fell over. Most of the time I just tried my best, kept my head up, and played the fat kid and ran straight into it, knocking it over with my belly!

I don't think it matters how you get past some of life's hurdles, just that you do eventually get past them. I just have to keep telling myself, "Maybe the next one will be shorter."

Before I had any of those hurdles, I had to figure out how to get out of my own way. I think many women have to figure this out. We all want the happily-ever-after so badly that we lose sight of the joy to be had in the here and now.

When you stop looking, you'll find it. Love. It finds you. I had stopped looking. I was happy with my "party of one".

I had a fun job, great friends, and a summer full of memories just waiting to be made in my midst. There were horses, tourists, and trail rides in my life during the day. At night, there were friends, rodeos, dancing and Long Islands on the patio.

Then it found me. Love, in a slightly tilted grey Cowboy hat with a half-cocked grin. The father of my unborn children. The maker of many memories. My partner. My sense of humor. My constant annoyance that I couldn't imagine not having. My life. My love. My Cowboy.

In a crowded Million Dollar Cowboy Bar, Love sat

down at my table. Love tipped his hat, shook my hand and introduced himself. I was intrigued.

When the band took a break from playing, it happened. The world stood still for a few moments. This cowboy leaned back in his chair during a silent moment so still you could hear a mouse fart. Then in a voice loud enough for at least half of the 500 patrons to hear, he proclaimed, "I'm DRUNK!...... I'm VULNERA-BLE!!.........and I @#$%&* on the FIRST DATE!!!"

After the surrounding people picked up their jaws from their firm position on the floor, laughter soon followed. I pounded my fist on the table between us. I had an urgent question for this man.

"Hey! Hey!" I shouted over the crowd, still pounding on the table. "HEY!"

He finally looked over at me and leaned in to see what all the fuss was about. With a stern face I asked, "How come that never works when I say it??"

A smile started to slip from the corner of my mouth. A slight chuckle from the Cowboy followed by a melt-your-knickers-off grin. He tipped the front of his hat slightly upwards, leaned in again and very matter-of-factly said, "Well, Sweetheart...that's because I've never been around."

We almost danced the night away. We then went to Village Inn to drink coffee and talk about our past, present and futures. We named our children over eggs and hash browns.

When the night was old and the next day was young, we walked outside. This cowboy then softly said, "I'm going to kiss you now." With a rough, manly hand placed gently on my cheek, we shared our last first kiss.

We soon parted ways because we had to go to work that morning. Later that evening, sitting on my front steps, I called home.

"Dad, I met the man I'm going to marry."

IF YOU LIKED THIS, YOU MIGHT LIKE: RANDOM THOUGHTS OF AN OLD WRITER

A MEMOIR BY ROBERT VAUGHAN

The autobiographical thoughts of award-winning author Robert Vaughan, start with his childhood, including a 71-year grudge against a bad call in a Little League Baseball game. Spanning across his time in the army, first as an enlisted man, to include his time as an aircraft maintenance instructor in the Army Aviation School at Rucker during which time he once wrestled a bear, and his time in Korea from a poignant Christmas, to finding an abandoned baby.

His military experiences also cover his time as a warrant officer, serving at Ft. Campbell, in Germany, where he engaged in a "slapping contest" with a German, three combat tours in Vietnam, including landing on a mine, being temporarily blinded, and scrounging a staff car from the Navy.

After leaving the army, Vaughan had a short, but active television career, from which he was fired for handcuffing the weather girl to a desk during a live broadcast. His TV career was followed by a stint of owning and publishing a newspaper, then, becoming a full time novelist with nearly 400 books published, including seven *New York Times* best-sellers. During his writing career, Vaughan was arrested by the FBI as a part of one of his books was read into the Watergate Hearings.

The book is told, not in numbered chapters, but in a series of titled vignettes.

AVAILABLE NOW

ABOUT THE AUTHOR

After spending most of her childhood living in Michigan, author Kacee Rundell moved back to her birthplace of Wyoming to study creative writing. While learning to craft her own voice on paper, she was surrounded by the farming and ranching culture.

Many years and four children later, she began to write again. This time it was far from fiction, but rather a documentation of a rare way of life that is slowly fading away on the winds of the timeless prairies, the American rancher. She fell in love with agriculture and felt a duty to share her experiences over the years.

These days Kacee still lives in her beautiful state of Wyoming with her children and small farming operation that keeps her busy at local farmers markets. As much as feeding cows is a necessity, so is writing. Her love of agriculture and writing will always collide as she sets her sights on moving back into the world of fiction.